Everything you want to know about Agile

How to get Agile results in a less-than-agile organization

Everything you want to know about Agile

How to get Agile results in a less-than-agile organization

JAMIE LYNN COOKE

IT Governance Publishing

Every possible effort has been made to ensure that the information contained in this book is accurate at the time of going to press, and the publisher and the author cannot accept responsibility for any errors or omissions, however caused. Any opinions expressed in this book are those of the author, not the publisher. Websites identified are for reference only, not endorsement, and any website visits are always at the reader's own risk. No responsibility for loss or damage occasioned to any person acting, or refraining from action, as a result of the material in this publication can be accepted by the publisher or the author.

PRINCE2® is a registered trade mark of the Cabinet Office. ITIL® is a registered trade mark of the Cabinet Office.

IT Governance Publishing
IT Governance Limited
Unit 3, Clive Court
Bartholomew's Walk
Cambridgeshire Business Park
Ely
Cambridgeshire
CB7 4EA
United Kingdom

www.itgovernance.co.uk

First published in the United Kingdom in 2012
by IT Governance Publishing.

ISBN 978-1-84928-323-6

DEDICATION

To my sister, Michele, for her insight and great advice.

FOREWORD

On a recent trip to the airport to catch a plane for my yearly vacation, I decided to use my new GPS with live traffic updates to plan the journey. Approximately halfway into the trip, the device alerted me to a potential problem and immediately recalculated a route, which got us to the airport with only a small delay of 10 minutes.

While we were sitting in the airport, we heard that the problem we had avoided was a multi-car accident on the highway, which resulted in airport traffic being delayed by over an hour, and several people missing their flights. We were extremely grateful for that piece of technology on the dashboard! It helped us to adjust our plans when circumstances changed, which allowed us to stay on track – and on time.

In traditional travel planning, you would get out an atlas, document the best route given the information that you had at hand, and then set out on the journey. You would then follow the route, putting your trust in the map and the plan that you had at the outset, with the belief that you would reach the required destination – and in the hope that you would do so in time. For the travel scenario above, following the traditional approach would have led us directly into the heart of the accident which, at the very least, would have caused us to miss the flight and spoiled my family vacation.

Fortunately for me, my GPS has an *Agile* approach to planning.

Foreword

Rather than planning a route and setting it in stone, the GPS planned *incrementally*, always working with the most current information available at the time. It regularly reviewed my progress against my objectives, and then used the incoming new knowledge to ensure that the route was still valid. As soon as a risk that would derail my objectives was identified, an alternative route to bring it back on track was devised and put into place. This eliminated the risk of failure and allowed the journey to stay on course. As each milestone was passed and a satisfactory result confirmed, the system recalculated the best plan for moving forward. This process was repeated throughout the journey, until I had achieved my goal.

From my perspective, it is clear that a GPS should be used whenever possible, as it is a far more efficient tool for navigation than traditional planning. So why does my father insist on using an atlas instead? The answer, is fear of change and the unknown.

Simply put, the atlas (i.e. traditional project management) is the way we have *always* done things. It has constantly been drummed into us that there is a need to plan, plan and plan again before embarking on a project; and that every eventuality and detail should be known, detailed and documented before making a move. The result is that the focus is always on the end goal, with the deliverable only being available – and assessed – at the last minute.

The problem with the traditional approach is that initial assumptions and information provided at the beginning of a project are invariably subject to change as a project progresses. By detailing everything at the start and being rigid about the product's delivery – with limited opportunity for sanity-checking or adjustment along the way – you risk ending up with a product that is completely unsuitable or, even worse, with a fully expended budget and *no* production-ready solution. Relying on upfront plans almost always results in huge costs for project rework and a delay in implementation that may be costly to both the business – and your reputation.

Agile project management tackles this by bringing a proven, flexible approach that *deliberately avoids* locking down finite detail at the outset. Instead, by collaborating with the customer to regularly deliver the most valuable outputs for the project, Agile replaces traditional upfront planning with *incremental* planning that incorporates the most current technical, market and business intelligence available. This not only ensures that the original project vision is intact, but that what the team delivers is at the right level of quality and is continually fit-for-purpose to support the overall goals. Agile approaches allow tangible business value to be delivered *throughout* the project, reinforcing senior management confidence in the project and in its delivery team along the way. Most important, Agile approaches can – and do – work in even the most traditional organizations.

In writing this book, Jamie has brought her extensive knowledge and experience to the fore, explaining in great detail not only the principles of Agile, but also the numerous methodologies that are available and how they might be applicable to your organization. By exploding the myths that Agile planning brings chaos – or that it cannot be integrated with existing methodologies, such as PRINCE2®, PMBOK® and ITIL®, with traditional budget management, or with traditional corporate reporting requirements – she removes many of the popular arguments that organizations have made for not implementing Agile in the first place. She shows that every IT department – even yours – is positioned to get the many benefits of Agile approaches.

In these current times of financial difficulty, when the focus is on providing more for less, this book makes a very compelling argument for the use of Agile in *every* organization, and I would recommend it without reservation.

Chris Evans MBCS DPSM

IT Service Management Specialist

PREFACE

Do you ever wonder why the software projects in your department consistently seem to run out of time or money (or both) before agreed goals have been achieved? Why staffing a team with technical experts and certified project managers is no guarantee of project success? Why what seemed like an achievable plan at the beginning of a software project inevitably falls short of expectations?

The Information Technology (IT) industry is filled with endless examples of high-visibility software projects that failed miserably: multi-million dollar budget blowouts, faulty software that was released prematurely into a live environment to meet a contractual (or management) deadline, and part-time support and maintenance services that become unending full-time commitments. Even more notorious are the numerous smaller projects, where delays, quality issues and firefighting eat away at staff's time, deplete allocated budgets, and risk jeopardizing the IT department's credibility in the organization.

The truth is that missed deadlines, problem-ridden software and budget blowouts have become so commonplace in the IT industry that people have come to expect them. It is a rare situation where software and IT services are delivered on time, within budget and to a sufficiently high quality to genuinely meet the needs of the business. Having an IT department that *consistently* achieves these objectives is virtually unheard of.

As an IT director, the challenges that you face in delivering successful software solutions and services are compounded exponentially by the challenges of achieving these objectives within the management structures and constraints of your organization – including budgeting, staffing, corporate reporting, complying with governance frameworks (e.g. PRINCE2® and ITIL®), strategic planning, negotiating and managing contracts, attending endless meetings, and keeping a range of internal and external stakeholders – including your executives – happy. This is *in addition* to the time that you spend fighting fires, addressing quality issues in delivered software, and appeasing dissatisfied users. These responsibilities alone are enough to fill a 60-hour week, which barely gives you breathing space to get your head around new approaches to software and services delivery, let alone implement them in your department. So why is Agile worth your time?

The best way to answer this question is by having a look at the *actual work* that your staff do on a daily basis. How much time do people really spend:

* Creating, adjusting – and maintaining – their project plans?
* Writing up – and then constantly modifying – functional and technical specification documents?
* Trying to interpret user requirements on their own (and then reworking released software to support what the users *actually* wanted)?
* Accommodating unrealistic – or unachievable – system capabilities that the users have requested?
* Building functionality that the business rarely – or never – uses?
* Managing scope creep when user requirements change (including corresponding changes to project plans, functional and technical specifications, resourcing, budgeting and contracts)?

- Firefighting to resolve last-minute issues before software is released?
- Addressing bug fixes and usability issues in the delivered software?

Each one of these activities is distracting your staff from the core business of delivering the systems and services that the business genuinely needs. These activities are eating away at your team's productivity by taking up an inordinate amount of their valuable time – and yours. A critical review of the day-to-day work in your department will likely reveal that the time-wasting activities listed above are the root cause of many of the missed deadlines and budget blowouts in your projects.

Agile methodologies provide *proven* and *practical* approaches for minimizing the countless hours that IT staff members spend on creating and updating upfront project plans, developing and maintaining detailed documentation, accommodating unrealistic user requirements, building low business-value features, and addressing pre- and post-production software problems. Agile approaches allow your staff to focus the majority of their time on building and delivering *high-quality, fully functional, fully tested* solutions that genuinely meet the needs of the business.

At the heart of Agile approaches are *adaptive management* practices that shift the focus of your staff from struggling with immovable upfront commitments to working *collaboratively* with business areas to achieve shared goals throughout the process. Agile replaces the time-consuming detailed management of scope creep with an understanding that user requirements *will change* as the project progresses, and, therefore, provides low-overhead structures to support these changes. Agile encourages teams to deliver *fully functional, fully tested, production-ready* software components on a regular basis (generally once a month), which mitigates the risk of finding significant technical issues at the end of the development cycle – when making changes to software can be much more costly and resource-intensive. Agile approaches measure the team's progress through hands-on reviews of *working software*, not piles of status reports.

These are the *real productivity gains[1]* that Agile approaches have delivered to thousands of organizations worldwide, including Nokia Siemens Networks[2], Yahoo![3], Google[4], Microsoft[5], BT[6], Bankwest[7], SunCorp[8] and Wells Fargo[9].

As an IT director, you are in a position to leverage the extensive work that these organizations have been doing

---

[1] See *www.realproductivitygains.com* for further details on identifying and quantifying real productivity gains.
[2] *NokiaSiemens and Agile Development*, Haapio P, JAOO (2008): *http://jaoo.dk/file?path=/jaoo-aarhus-2008/slides//PetriHaapio_CanAGLobalCompany.pdf*.
[3] *Lessons from a Yahoo Scrum Rollout*, Mackie K (2008): *http://campustechnology.com/articles/2008/02/lessons-from-a-yahoo-scrum-rollout.aspx*.
[4] *Scrum Tuning: Lessons Learned from Scrum implementation at Google*, Sutherland J (2006): *http://video.google.com/videoplay?docid=8795214308797356840&q=type%3Agoogle+engEDU*.
[5] *Microsoft Lauds Scrum Method for Software Projects*, Taft D K (2005): *www.eweek.com/c/a/IT-Management/Microsoft-Lauds-Scrum-Method-for-Software-Projects/*.
[6] *Agile Coaching in British Telecom*, Meadows L and Hanly S (2006): *www.agilejournal.com/articles/columns/column-articles/144-agile-coaching-in-british-telecom*.
[7] *Bankwest goes agile: project time slashed (2010)*: *www.zdnet.com.au/bankwest-goes-agile-project-time-slashed-339306091.htm*.
[8] *Suncorp goes Agile for 19k desktop integration project* (2008): *www.itnews.com.au/News/130927,suncorp-goes-agile-for-19k-desktop-integration-project.aspx*.
[9] *Ready, Fire, Aim! An Agile Approach to Architecture & Software Development* (2009): *www.milwaukeeagile.com/events/11787272/?eventId=11787272&action=detail*.

over the past 20 years to implement – and refine – Agile approaches. However, the real challenge for you is to make these approaches work within the structures, constraints and culture of *your* organization.

This book has been written specifically to address the unique challenges that IT directors and managers face when implementing Agile approaches within their organizations. It provides you with the information that you need to assess whether Agile is right for your department, to select the Agile methodologies and practices that are best suited to the work that you do, to successfully implement these approaches in your department, and to measure the outcomes. Most importantly, this book gives you strategies for aligning Agile work within the unique reporting, budgeting, staffing and governance constraints of your organization – arguably, the biggest challenge.

ABOUT THE AUTHOR

Jamie Lynn Cooke has 21 years of experience as a senior business analyst and solutions consultant, working with over 125 public and private sector organizations throughout Australia, Canada and the United States.

Her background includes business case development; strategic and operational reviews; business process modeling, mapping and optimization; product and project management on small to multi-million dollar initiatives; quality management; risk analysis and mitigation; developing/conducting training courses; workshop delivery; and refining e-business strategies.

She is the author of *Agile Productivity Unleashed: Proven approaches for achieving real productivity gains*, IT Governance Publishing (2010) – a book written specifically to explain Agile in non-technical business terms to managers and executives outside of the IT industry. She is also the author of *Agile: An Executive Guide – Real results from IT budgets*, IT Governance Publishing (2011) which gives IT executives the tools and strategies needed for making bottom-line business decisions on using Agile methodologies.

She is a well-regarded speaker on both business and technology topics, most recently presenting on issues such as *Getting Management and Customer Support for Using Agile* and *When is Agile Not the Answer?* at the Business Process Modeling world conference in Brisbane, Australia and at the AgileCanberra professional forums.

About the Author

Jamie has been working hands-on with Agile methodologies since 2003, and has researched hundreds of books and articles on Agile topics. She is a signatory to the Agile Manifesto, has attended numerous Agile seminars; and has worked with prominent consultants to promote Agile methodologies to large organizations.

Jamie has a Bachelor of Science in Engineering Psychology (Human Factors Engineering) from Tufts University in Medford, Massachusetts, and a Graduate Certificate in e-Business/Business Informatics from the University of Canberra in Australia.

ACKNOWLEDGEMENTS

My continued thanks to the pioneers and thought leaders of the Agile world – most notably Kent Beck, Martin Fowler, Alistair Cockburn, Jeff Sutherland, Mike Cohn, Ken Schwaber and Jim Highsmith – for their passionate work in developing and refining Agile methodologies over the past two decades. Particular thanks go to Artem Marchenko of *www.AgileSoftwareDevelopment.com*[10] for generously making his tracking tools available for everyone in the Agile community to use.

Thanks also to the small and large organizations worldwide that have allowed their experiences in using Agile to be shared with others, including Nokia Siemens Networks, Yahoo!, Google, Microsoft and BT.

Special thanks to Neil Salkind of the Salkind Literary Agency and Angela Wilde of IT Governance Publishing for their ongoing support and sage advice.

We would like to acknowledge and thank the following reviewers of this book for their very useful contributions: Robin Smith, Head of Information Risk, UHL NHS and Jared Carstensen, Manager, Deloitte & Touche.

Many thanks, as well, to the people who taught me most about the strategies of the business world over the past 21 years, especially Roland Scornavacca, Tony Robey and Peter Walsh; to Rowan Bunning for being an unending source of Agile knowledge; to Chris Evans for his

---

[10] *www.agilesoftwaredevelopment.com.*

Acknowledgements

extremely valuable input; and to the writers and teachers who inspired me – particularly Richard Leonard[11], for his amazing ability to encourage writers with his humor and enthusiasm.

Finally, my eternal gratitude to my parents, my US family, my Australian family and my friends – most especially Susan, Michele, Janice, Elissa and Linda – for continuing to be my sanity check in this world. Most of all, thank you to my husband, David, for 20 years of love and laughter.

---

[11] Richard Leonard's website: *www.richardleonard.net.*

CONTENTS

Contents

Contents

Contents

INTRODUCTION

The *Harvard Business Journal* recently advised that the successful delivery of IT initiatives is a joint responsibility between the people who develop solutions and the business areas that require those solutions[12]:

"Success requires a sustained commitment for the managers who will use and benefit from the initiative, not just IT."

Agile approaches are built around the very concept of collaborative work between IT staff and business areas; however, Agile takes the idea further by advocating that the *only* way to truly know whether IT initiatives are consistently meeting business requirements is to *actively involve* the business area (the "customer") in the regular review and refinement of *fully functional, fully tested* system capabilities. Agile works on the premise that detailed user requirements specification documents and prototype screens are *no substitute* for getting direct feedback from the customer's *hands-on review* of *working capabilities* in their solutions. Equally, there is no better way to measure quality, relevance and progress than having the project team consistently deliver fully functional, fully tested, production-ready software capabilities.

As an IT director, you know that staff can spend as much – if not more – of their time *reworking* delivered software

---

[12] *Don't Blame IT for that Failed Initiative* (2011): http://hbr.org/tip?date=072511.

than they spent developing the original solution. One of the greatest advantages of allowing customers to review fully functional capabilities *during the development process* is that it provides them with the opportunity to see how the business requirements that they envisaged *actually* behave. This allows them to adjust system functionality, screen layouts and business rules to most effectively meet their needs *while the solution is being developed* (i.e. the time when your staff will be able to implement these changes more quickly, with fewer overhead costs, and less risk to the overall system). It means that the solution that your staff deliver will be more valuable to the business, more likely to be accepted for production release, and more likely to result in satisfied users. However, the benefits of Agile approaches extend far beyond the significant reduction in time that your staff will spend reworking solutions at the end of the development life cycle.

IT projects traditionally include endless piles of planning and specification documents that need to be created before development work on a project can even begin. Although creating these documents can be a very time-consuming activity, it often pales in comparison to the amount of time that staff spend *reworking* them as the project progresses to accommodate:

- Adjustments to system capabilities based on constraints found during software development
- Updated business requirements based on changes that occur *within* the organization (e.g. new management directives, staff departures, funding reallocations)
- Updated business requirements based on changes that occur *external* to the organization (e.g. fluctuations in market demand, announcements from competitors, the availability of new technologies)

- User requests to change system behavior as a result of acceptance testing
- User requests to change system behavior after it has been released in the live environment.

No amount of detailed planning – even by the most experienced IT resources – can accurately predict the changes that will occur during the course of a project. This is why Agile approaches replace upfront planning with *incremental planning* based on the collaborative work between the project team and the customer. Working jointly with the customer provides staff with an ongoing opportunity to *more easily adapt* solutions (and supporting documentation) to reflect the changes that occur within the organization – and external to the organization – as the project progresses. It enables your staff to refocus their day-to-day efforts on *delivering outcomes* instead of endless documentation, and to focus on *incremental planning* instead of spending time making retrospective adjustments to originally agreed upfront project plans.

This focus on high productivity is also why Agile approaches require project teams to produce *fully functional, fully tested, production-ready* software throughout the project. This allows the project team to identify – and resolve – technical and usability issues as early in the process as possible.

The end result is that Agile approaches enable staff to shift from a heavy reliance on the inaccuracies of *predictive* development work to the efficiencies of *emergent* development work that is aligned with the ongoing needs of the organization. This would be an ideal model, were it not for the fact that most organizations manage their work in exactly the opposite way.

One of the greatest difficulties in successfully implementing Agile approaches comes from the fact that organizations generally structure their overall operations around *upfront planning*. Annual reports, yearly budget allocations, business plans, sales forecasts, marketing plans and staffing strategies are generally developed well before the scheduled work is undertaken. Departments are expected to reasonably estimate (i.e. *predict*) their workloads, budget utilization, resourcing requirements and outputs at the start of the reporting cycle; and managers are then measured by how well the actual work undertaken meets their original estimations. No matter how productive Agile approaches are for IT initiatives, they still need to fit within the core constraints of the overall organization. So, how does an approach that is based on adapting work as it progresses fit within an organizational environment that is based almost exclusively on upfront commitments? Answering that question is the core objective of this book.

Chapters 1 to 6 provide you with background information on Agile approaches, including:

- The historical issues in the IT industry that led to the emergence of Agile
- The business benefits that the approaches can provide for your department
- The most common Agile methodologies
- Organizations worldwide that actively use Agile approaches.

Chapters 7 to 11 give you the information that you need to determine if Agile is right for your department, to select the Agile approaches that are best suited to meet your specific needs, and to successfully introduce, implement and monitor Agile approaches within your department.

Chapters 12 to 18 provide you with guidance on how to implement Agile work within the specific constraints of your organization, including your existing:

- Governance structures, such as PRINCE2®, PMBOK®, CMMI® and ITIL® (*see Chapter 13: Managing Agile within Your Existing Project Frameworks*)
- Fixed budget allocations (*see Chapter 14: Budgeting for Agile Work*)
- Corporate reporting requirements (*see Chapter 15: Reporting on Agile Projects*)
- Contractual commitments (*see Chapter 16: Establishing Agile Contracts*)
- Staffing procedures (*see Chapter 17: Building the Right Agile Team and Chapter 18: Conducting Performance Reviews for Agile Teams*).

Each of these chapters presents the ideal model of how each function would be structured in an optimal environment (i.e. in an organization that is built around adaptive management), and then provides guidelines for how the remaining 99% of readers can deliver Agile results in their less-than-agile organizational environments.

Once you have determined the best way to make Agile work within your department – and your organization – *Chapters 19 and 20* offer some additional advice to help you successfully implement Agile, including tips on how to avoid the most common Agile traps and how to expand the use of Agile over time.

Finally, *Chapter 21* provides you with a range of additional resources for your reference, including more detailed information on the specific Agile methodologies that you may be interested in.

The information in this book is designed to provide you with a comprehensive foundation of the strategies and tools that you need to make Agile a reality in your department – and your organization.

CHAPTER 1: WHAT IS AGILE? [13]

"Agile" is a collective term for methodologies (and practices) that have emerged over the past two decades to increase the relevance, quality, flexibility and business value of software solutions. These *adaptive management* approaches are specifically intended to address the problems that have historically plagued software development and service delivery activities in the IT industry – including budget overruns, missed deadlines, low-quality outputs, and dissatisfied users.

Although there is a broad range of Agile methodologies in the IT industry – from software development and project delivery approaches to strategies for software maintenance – all Agile methodologies share the same basic objectives:

- To *replace upfront planning with incremental planning* that adapts to the most current information available (i.e. the "apply, inspect, adapt" mindset)
- To *build in quality upfront* and then relentlessly confirm the integrity of the solution throughout the process
- To *address technical risks as early in the process as possible* to reduce the potential for these resulting in cost and time blowouts as the project progresses
- To *minimize the impact of changing requirements* by providing a low overhead structure to accommodate

---

[13] For those who follow this author's writing, some of the introductory material from *Agile: An Executive Guide – Real results from IT budgets*, Jamie Lynn Cooke, IT Governance Publishing (2011) has been adapted for use in this book, serving the same purpose as in the original.

variations to the originally-identified requirements throughout the project

- To *deliver frequent and continuous business value to the organization* by focusing staff on regularly delivering the highest-priority features in the solution as fully functional, fully tested, production-ready capabilities

> **Agile methodologies** are common-sense approaches for applying the finite resources of an organization to continuously deliver low-risk, high business-value software solutions

- To *entrust and empower staff* to continuously deliver high business-value outputs
- To *encourage ongoing communication between the business areas and project team members* to increase the relevance, usability, quality and acceptance of delivered solutions.

Some of the most common Agile methodologies (also referred to as "Agile methods") include:

- Iterative strategies for managing software development projects, such as Scrum, the Dynamic Systems Development Method (DSDM), Feature Driven Development™ (FDD™), the Agile Unified Process (AUP) and Lean Development
- Strategies for optimizing software development work, such as eXtreme Programming™ (XP) and the Rational Unified Process® (RUP®)

- Strategies for managing software maintenance and support activities, such as Kanban.[14]

These Agile methodologies have been (and continue to be) successfully used by thousands of organizations worldwide[15] – most notably in the United States and Europe. Some of the more prominent organizations using Agile methodologies include Nokia Siemens Networks, Yahoo!, Google, Microsoft, BT, Bankwest and SunCorp.

It is interesting to note the breadth of industries that these organizations represent – from high technology to finance to telecommunications. Equally noteworthy is the fact that these are not start-up organizations – most have been established for decades. Most importantly, these are organizations that are subject to the same drivers and constraints as your organization: revenue generation, service provision, annual reports, shareholders, public relations, competitive positioning and strategic planning. Not only do these organizations make Agile work within their corporate structures, they actually use Agile to more effectively achieve their organization's objectives[16].

In order to fully appreciate the effectiveness of Agile methodologies, it is worthwhile taking a couple of minutes to understand the business environment that caused these methodologies to be established in the first place.

---

[14] Further detail on each of these methodologies is provided in *Chapter 4: Common Agile Methodologies at a Glance.*
[15] As evidenced by the number of signatories to the Agile Manifesto (*www.agilemanifesto.org*) as at December 2011.
[16] In several cases, these organizations even publish case studies to demonstrate their success in using Agile approaches, such as those referenced in the Preface.

CHAPTER 2: A FIVE-MINUTE HISTORY OF AGILE

In the 1990s, the IT industry was plagued by the remarkably high failure rate of software development projects: projects that became notorious for their missed deadlines, substantially overrun budgets, faulty deliverables and dissatisfied customers. A handful of thought leaders in the industry believed that these IT project failures could be attributed to three key factors: over-planning, insufficient communication and "all-at-once" delivery.

Over-planning

IT software projects traditionally began with the production of extensive upfront documentation, which included project plans, functional requirements, system design specifications and technical architectural designs. These documents – which often took months to produce (and even longer to get approved) – were intended to ensure that the developed software would align with user requirements. In reality, however, these documents only served to provide corporate managers with a false sense of security in the expenditure of their IT budgets, and to ensure that delivered software would be substantially misaligned with the ongoing – and changing – needs of the business.

The biggest problems with organizations relying upon upfront documentation were:

* The resulting lack of responsiveness to ongoing changes in user requirements, market demand, internal resource availability and the capabilities of the underlying technologies

- The tendency for stakeholders (e.g. business areas and customers) to:
  - ○ Not clearly articulate their requirements (which were then left to the discretion of the project team to interpret)
  - ○ Want everything under the sun (resulting in highly critical business requirements being lost in a sea of extraneous requirements).
- The inevitable misalignment between text descriptions of the users' needs and the resulting software.

The bottom line is that software products delivered to meet these upfront design documents were destined to fail – and businesses were losing millions in the process.

Insufficient communication

The second overwhelming driver in the ongoing failure of software development projects in the 1990s was the traditional – and often deliberate – separation between the business areas that required the software and the technical staff responsible for delivering the solution (i.e. development in a vacuum).

Once the big upfront design documents for an IT project had been finalized, they were generally handed over to the project team for development. The project team was then sent back to their desks (often located in a separate section, floor or even building from the business areas), with a pile of paper and an immutable deadline. The next time that the project team interacted with the business area was when they installed the resulting software on the users' machines for acceptance testing.

This isolation created inevitable issues with the resulting software because:

- User requirements had been left to the interpretation of the project team members without the benefit of understanding the business context
- The inevitable disconnect between the two-dimensional concept proposed in the documentation and the manifestation of that concept into tangible screens that the user could interact with
- No allowance had been made for changes in business requirements that may have occurred between the time that the user was last consulted and the months (and sometimes years) that followed before the resulting software was installed on their system.

All of these factors resulted in the delivery of software that was frequently misaligned with the needs of the business users and included inadequate workflows, system errors, critical design flaws and features that were rarely (or never) used by the business. On top of this, there was no remaining budget or resources available to address any of the issues.

"All-at-once" delivery

Software development projects in the 1990s depended heavily on "waterfall" project management methodologies, where analysis, design, development, testing and delivery stages were undertaken serially, requiring the full completion of one activity before the next one could begin. The use of waterfall methodologies on these projects meant that software design could not begin until all of the requirements analysis was complete, software testing could not begin until software development was complete, and software was not delivered to the users until all of the preceding stages had been completed.

This use of waterfall approaches in the IT industry was intended to reduce business risk in project delivery by requiring each step to be completed to management's satisfaction before further expenditure was incurred. In reality, waterfall approaches significantly *increased* the risk of IT project failure by:

- Mandating big upfront documentation (with all of its related issues)
- Discouraging responsiveness to changing requirements as the project evolved
- Creating "silos" of ownership that reduced communication across project team members.

Perhaps the most risky impact of these waterfall approaches was the delaying of the delivery of tangible business outcomes until the very end of the project – the point at which problems in the software are the most evident and changes to the software are most costly.

Instead of enabling the organization to manage expenditures and risks throughout the software development process, executives were faced with an all-or-nothing proposition: keep pouring resources into a failing IT project – so that at least some value can be recovered from the previous investment – or end the project midstream and receive no tangible benefit to the organization. The "all-at-once" delivery approach often left these executives with no other options.

There were, of course, other factors that influenced the high failure rate of software development projects in the 1990s, including limitations in technology and the lack of availability of skilled technical resources. However, the three issues outlined above – over-planning, insufficient communication and "all-at-once" delivery – were factors that were *within the control of the organization to change.*

In order to combat the widespread failure of IT projects, a group of innovative thought leaders began to develop strategies and practices that were specifically designed to address these three issues. It is their insight, along with the contributions of many others who followed, which has resulted in the proven, business-value-driven Agile methodologies that are used throughout the world today.

CHAPTER 3: THE CORE BUSINESS BENEFITS OF AGILE

IT directors are in a unique position to align the day-to-day work that is done by their staff with the overarching strategic objectives and guidelines of the organization. This combined role can often be a balancing act of juggling executive demands along with the practical challenges of delivering effective technology solutions. However, it also provides an opportunity for IT directors to *double* the benefits that they can receive from the use of Agile approaches in their department by leveraging both the *strategic* and *tactical* advantages that they deliver.

At a *strategic* level, Agile benefits include:

- **Ongoing risk management:** This is achieved by regularly confirming and adjusting requirements according to ongoing interactions with the customer[17] and by delivering fully functional and fully tested software features, so that technical risks are identified and mitigated throughout the process.
- **Ongoing control of budget expenditure:** This is achieved by providing decision makers with the opportunity to review and assess the business value of deliverables at each iteration, and with the option to adjust, postpone or stop ongoing funding based on the return on investment (ROI) of delivered work.

---

[17] Where the "customer" is the business area requiring the solution – which could be another department within your organization, or an external client.

- **Rapid delivery of tangible outcomes:** This is achieved by focusing team efforts on regularly producing fully functional, fully tested, production-ready software features that can be used by the organization well before the end of the project timeline.
- **Strong alignment with business requirements:** This is maintained by directly involving the customer in the initial and ongoing review of developed software, and by incorporating their feedback throughout the process.
- **Focus on the highest-priority features:** This is maintained by continually working with the customer to confirm and adjust the work undertaken by the project team to align with the most current priorities of the organization.
- **Responsiveness to business change:** This is achieved by adjusting work throughout the process to incorporate organizational, industry and technology changes.
- **Transparency in status tracking:** This is achieved by regularly providing tangible outputs for customer review, combined with the use of open communication forums and centrally available real-time status-tracking tools.
- **Substantially higher-quality outputs:** This is achieved by incorporating rigid testing regimes throughout the process and by working regularly with the customer to confirm the usability and business value of delivered features.
- **Greater employee retention:** This is achieved by creating work environments that are based on high communication, empowering the team, trusting their

expertise, encouraging innovation, and regularly acknowledging their contribution to the organization[18].

* **Minimized whole-of-life software costs:** This is achieved by incorporating usability, quality and extensibility into solutions throughout the delivery process – thereby reducing both development costs and support and maintenance overheads – and by providing a less risky and more cost-effective platform for additional functionality to be integrated into the solutions.

Interestingly, each of the strategic benefits of Agile approaches listed above can also deliver equivalent *tactical* benefits for you and your staff:

* **The production of more valuable outputs per resource hour:** Strategic benefits, such as the *focus on the highest-priority features, ongoing risk management* and producing *substantially higher-quality outputs,* can result in significantly more effective use of staff time. This means that your department can produce more business value for the same level of effort, and within the same timeframe and budget. Higher levels of productivity during standard working hours also minimize the need for last-minute firefighting and overtime.

* **Earlier identification of technical issues:** The *rapid delivery of tangible outcomes* as part of *ongoing risk management* compels staff to regularly produce fully functional and fully tested features. Building these functional capabilities requires working system

---

[18] From the staff member's perspective, this collaborative and supportive work environment is arguably the most important business benefit of using Agile approaches.

components, such as an established architecture, a live database, and a functional integration platform – all of which can help with the identification of technical risks for isolated features well before they become whole-of-solution issues.

- **Less rework and "throw-away" work:** The *strong alignment with business requirements, focus on the highest-priority features,* and *responsiveness to business change* that underpin Agile approaches at a strategic level also serve to focus staff on consistently producing capabilities that the business *actually* needs with features that are usable – *and used* – by the customer. Not only does this create a stronger working relationship with the customer (and more positive feedback about your department throughout the organization), it also means that customers are less likely to urgently need critical features added to a delivered system (i.e. less firefighting and fewer last-minute demands on your department).

- **Reduced need to create – and maintain – detailed documentation:** The *rapid delivery of tangible outcomes, strong alignment with business requirements,* and *responsiveness to business change* all serve to reduce the organization's dependency on having requirements documented in detail before development work can begin. Business users quickly learn to trust the process – and the team – to deliver capabilities that meet their requirements, rather than rely upon pre-defined documentation as a "safety net" to ensure that their needs will be met. In addition, *transparency in status tracking* means that the department will be less dependent upon detailed upfront project plans (and ongoing adaptations to these plans) as a way of ensuring that work stays on track to deliver agreed outcomes.

- **Greater flexibility:** Both the *rapid delivery of tangible outcomes* and *responsiveness to business change* mean that solutions, by necessity, need to be easily extensible to minimize overheads when changes are inevitably required. However, the flexibility provided by Agile approaches goes far beyond technical flexibility; the incremental planning process provides management flexibility in the *ongoing control of budget expenditure* by allowing decision makers to regularly review and adjust work to meet the highest-priority demands of the department (which could include re-assigning staff to other high priority work as needed).
- **More staff autonomy:** *Ongoing risk management, rapid delivery of tangible outcomes,* and *transparency in status tracking* all mean that the results of Agile work will be apparent to management without the need for constant staff supervision. This is coupled with the benefits provided through the *strong alignment with business requirements*, which means that the work delivered by staff will be regularly reviewed and confirmed by the customer. All of this allows both staff and management to focus on their core responsibilities, which can result in the more efficient use of the department's limited resources.
- **Greater job satisfaction:** The *rapid delivery of tangible outcomes* provides staff with a far greater sense of accomplishment in their work than they can get from producing piles of documentation. This is coupled with the delivery of *substantially higher-quality outputs,* resulting in staff taking greater pride in the work that they deliver. Overall, this can result in an environment of *greater employee retention,* with the corresponding

benefits of reducing the department's overhead in replacing staff and preserving corporate memory.

- **Greater opportunity for innovation:** An environment that fosters the *rapid delivery of tangible outcomes,* the production of *substantially higher-quality outputs* and *responsiveness to business change* requires staff to be creative in the design of their solutions to ensure that delivered functionality and underlying technical platforms are readily adaptable in the future. This can often lead to innovative – if not cutting-edge – solutions to address the challenges of ensuring both utility and extensibility in delivered capabilities.

- **Reduced dependency on paper status reports:** *Rapid delivery of tangible outcomes, ongoing risk management* and *transparency in status tracking* all combine to reduce the department's dependency on staff to produce paper-based status reports. Instead, progress is measured by the production of outputs, the customer's response to delivered capabilities, and the team's use of real-time tracking tools. The organization as a whole may still require the department to provide paper-based status updates (*see Chapter 15: Reporting on Agile Projects*), but you and your staff do not need to add to this compliance burden by producing endless reports *within* the department.

- **Reduced demand for ongoing support and maintenance:** The *strong alignment with business requirements, focus on the highest-priority features, responsiveness to business change* and *delivery of substantially higher-quality outputs* all combine to minimize whole-of-life software costs for the solutions that your department delivers. Systems are thoroughly tested and confirmed by the business users well before they are released into a production environment. This does not mean that the solutions that your staff deliver will be 100% error free – or that evolving business demands will not result in the need for future enhancements. Instead, it means that quality control throughout the Agile development process – combined with the inherent extensibility of delivered solutions – can substantially minimize your department's time and cost overheads in maintaining live solutions.

The following section provides an overview of some of the most common Agile methodologies, so that you can begin to see which of them may be best suited to deliver the benefits just described within the specific requirements (and constraints) of your department.

CHAPTER 4: COMMON AGILE METHODOLOGIES AT A GLANCE

Scrum

Scrum is an iterative project management methodology that is most commonly used for Agile software development projects, but is suitable for any project-based work. Scrum provides a framework for business areas to identify and prioritize work required, and for project teams to commit to the subset of priority items they believe can be delivered in each two- to four-week iteration (or "sprint").

Scrum requires the nomination of resources to fulfill key roles in the project, including:

• **The Product Owner:** who represents the needs of the business and is responsible for documenting and prioritizing high-level requirements as input into ongoing planning
• **The Scrum Team:** a cross-disciplinary team charged with undertaking the agreed work in each sprint
• **The ScrumMaster:** who facilitates the team's work by removing project impediments and ensuring that appropriate Scrum practices are being followed by the team.

Core to the success of Scrum are two activities that are undertaken at each iterative sprint:

• **The sprint planning meeting**: held at the beginning of each sprint; this is where the Product Owner, ScrumMaster and Scrum Team review the highest-priority items identified by the Product Owner and agree on the subset of priority items that will be included in the forthcoming sprint

- **The sprint review**: held at the end of each sprint; this includes a demonstration of work completed in that sprint and a retrospective review of the work undertaken to enable continuous improvement for subsequent iterations.

Scrum also encourages project teams to engage in daily stand-up meetings: short update sessions held each morning that enable the team to quickly review required work and address any hurdles.

The progress of the Scrum Team's work is communicated to stakeholders through monitoring and measurement tools, such as the:

> **Scrum**® is an Agile methodology for project management that involves:
>
> - Delivering software in time-boxed iterations
> - Focusing on the highest business-value software features in each iteration
> - Interacting directly with business users to confirm ongoing software usability, quality, relevance and business value throughout the process.

- **Executive dashboard:** a report that summarizes the work within (and across) Agile teams for easy progress monitoring across the department
- **Product backlog:** a reporting tool that enables both stakeholders and project teams to monitor the progress of work against the agreed business requirements

- **Sprint backlog:** a reporting tool that enables project teams to monitor and manage their actual day-to-day work.

Scrum is arguably the most commonly used Agile approach worldwide, and a range of professional courses are available to certify people for roles, such as the ScrumMaster and Product Owner. These courses foster the consistent and effective application of these roles in every organization. They are also intended to address common areas of misapplication in Scrum implementations, such the mistaken view of the ScrumMaster as a project manager (instead of a facilitator).

Feature Driven Development™ (FDD™)

Feature Driven Development™ is an Agile methodology that combines elements of iterative project management with practices that are specific to software development. The basic driver of FDD™ is to provide incremental value to the business by delivering complete, working product capabilities (i.e. software "features" and "feature sets") in every iteration.

FDD™ requires close collaboration with the business areas to establish an upfront "domain model" of the business problem that the proposed system is intended to address. Once this domain model has been identified, it is broken down (decomposed) into smaller units (i.e. "features"), which can then be developed and delivered iteratively. Team members are then assigned to build nominated features that, once successfully tested, are incorporated into the larger system.

In many respects, FDD™ works according to the same underlying principles as other Agile methodologies (e.g. Scrum), in that the project team works closely with the business areas to deliver regular, incremental value to the organization. However, FDD™ is far more prescriptive about defining the boundaries of the solution upfront, assigning specific roles and

Feature Driven Development™ **(FDD**™**)** is an Agile methodology that combines iterative project delivery with software development practices by:

- Having teams model the business problem upfront
- Decomposing the model into smaller features and feature sets
- Integrating selected feature sets into the overall software solution through iterative releases
- Keeping a strong focus on collaboration with users, production of tangible outputs, and quality management throughout the process.

responsibilities to the project team members, and controlling the scope of each team member's work during the actual software development process.

Based on the above, it is argued that, although FDD™ delivers most of the strategic and tactical benefits identified in *Chapter 3: The Core Business Benefits of Agile*, its ability to deliver *responsiveness to business change* is limited. This is because the structure of FDD™ makes it less responsive to ongoing organizational, industry or technology changes that do not fit in with the originally-identified domain model.

eXtreme Programming™ (XP)

eXtreme Programming™ (XP) is an activity-specific Agile methodology for iterative software development work. XP encourages software developers to produce and deliver the *simplest possible technical solution* required to meet the customer's objectives, *anticipates that requirements will change* once the customer has had an opportunity to work with the delivered software, and encourages the *ongoing improvement and optimization of the software* based on customer feedback.

Unlike the "big upfront documentation" approaches that burdened the IT industry in the 1990s, XP documents business requirements at a high level – and then works *hands-on* with the customer to deliver their desired outcomes using the simplest designs, delivered in the earliest possible timeframes.

XP incorporates the use of an Agile practice called *Test-Driven Development* (TDD), which encourages software developers to create the tests that will be used to validate the code that they are building *prior to* undertaking development work. TDD is an innovative quality management approach that requires project team members to define and document their measures of success prior to undertaking the work required.

Another Agile practice used in XP is a concept known as *refactoring*, which allows the team to regularly review the existing system and modify it – where required – so that future software changes can be implemented more easily. Amazingly, this includes full authority for the team to *throw away* existing software in favor of a replacement solution that will provide the organization with greater flexibility to address future requirements. XP advocates that the short-term loss of work undertaken is worth the long-term opportunity for software solutions to grow with the organization.

XP also utilizes a number of other Agile practices that enable staff to regularly deliver high-quality outputs and reduce ongoing maintenance costs, including:

> **eXtreme Programming**™ **(XP)** is an Agile methodology for software development work that is based on:
>
> * Delivering the *simplest possible technical solution* required to meet the customer's objectives
> * Anticipating that *requirements will change* once the customer has had an opportunity to work with the delivered software
> * Encouraging the *ongoing improvement and optimization of the software* based on customer feedback.

* **Pair programming:** having two members of the project team work together on assigned tasks to increase accountability and knowledge sharing
* **Automated testing:** using an automated testing harness (or equivalent) to regularly confirm the integrity of developed software – in particular, to see if code changes have impacted other functions in the solution
* **Continuous integration:** integrating newly developed code into the code base of the working system, so that updated capabilities are continuously available for production release. Note that continuous integration is generally used *in conjunction with* automated testing to ensure that updated code has not introduced errors into the existing system.

The iterative and customer-driven nature of XP enables it to deliver most of the strategic and tactical benefits identified in *Chapter 3: The Core Business Benefits of Agile*; however, as XP is not a formal project management methodology[19], it can only influence ongoing budget management with decision makers indirectly through customer feedback (or in combination with other Agile methodologies, such as Scrum).

It is the simplicity of design, the focus on quality, the expectation of change and the freedom afforded to the team to rethink and optimize software solutions that make XP one of the most well-regarded and widely used Agile methodologies.

Dynamic Systems Development Method (DSDM)

The Dynamic Systems Development Method (DSDM) framework is another iterative approach to managing Agile software development projects that has its roots in Rapid Application Development (RAD), resulting in a strong emphasis on building prototypes and confirming the feasibility of the solution with the business prior to undertaking full development activities. This is evidenced by DSDM requiring stakeholder workshops, a feasibility report, a feasibility prototype and a business study to be undertaken prior to full implementation.

---

[19] Noting that there is an emerging interest in using the powerful techniques of XP for eXtreme Project Management.

The practices that underpin DSDM are at the very heart of Agile methodologies, including active user involvement throughout the process, iterative and incremental development, frequent delivery of tangible outputs and empowering the

> The **Dynamic Systems Development Method (DSDM®)** is an Agile methodology for project delivery that involves:
>
> • Delivering software in time-boxed iterations
> • Prototyping and documenting the software solution prior to undertaking full development activities
> • Collaborating with users, producing tangible outputs, and ensuring quality management throughout the process.

team. Ongoing testing and quality control of software throughout the process are also emphasized.

Unlike Scrum, however, the DSDM framework requires a range of artifacts (e.g. development plans and functional models) to be developed at each phase of the project, which provide ongoing confirmation that planned work is aligned with the needs of the business.

Although the approaches differ, both Scrum and DSDM have the same core objective – the delivery of high business-value outcomes in controlled, iterative timeframes. Scrum provides a high-level framework for achieving this objective, and relies on communication between the participants to ensure that work undertaken meets ongoing business needs. DSDM provides a more structured framework to achieve this objective, requiring proposed work to be documented and confirmed prior to continuing to the next stage.

Lean Development

Lean Development (Lean) is an Agile methodology that combines elements of iterative project management with best practices in software design and development. Lean stems from the Lean manufacturing processes that originated as early as 1922[20], but most closely aligns with the principles in KAIZEN[21] and Total Quality Management (TQM).[22]

At the heart of Lean is value stream mapping, focusing on:

* Identifying and confirming the business value of customer requirements
* Delivering the highest business-value software features
* Making software development processes as efficient as possible.

As a corollary to this, Lean promotes the identification and elimination of *areas of waste* within the software development process (e.g. project teams unable to progress their work because they are waiting for input from the business).

---

[20] *My Life and Work,* Ford H with Crowther S, Garden City Publishing Company, Inc. (1922), ISBN 9781406500189.
[21] *KAIZEN – The Japanese Strategy for Continuous Improvement,* Kotelnikov V (last updated November 9th, 2010)
www.1000ventures.com/business_guide/mgmt_kaizen_main.html.
[22] *Total Quality Management (TQM) – An Integrated Approach to Quality and Continuous Improvement,* Kotelnikov V (last updated January 27th, 2011)
www.1000ventures.com/business_guide/im_tqm_main.html.

Another core principle of Lean is fast delivery (deriving from queuing theory and just-in-time practices), which encourages project teams to:

- Use *pull* techniques to respond to customer needs as they emerge
- Align the volume and complexity of their work with their optimal capacity to deliver.

In support of this, Lean encourages the team to hold off on making decisions for as long as is reasonably possible in the software

Lean Development (Lean) is an Agile methodology that combines elements of iterative project management with best practices in software design and development by:

- Using value stream mapping to deliver the highest business-value features within the most efficient software development process
- Incorporating pull techniques and optimal capacity planning to deliver results as quickly as possible
- Enforcing stringent quality management through integrity checking and continuous improvement
- Empowering skilled cross-functional teams to deliver the highest-value outcomes to the department.

development process to provide maximum flexibility in addressing ongoing business requirements.

Lean also incorporates stringent quality management techniques by enforcing system integrity at both the business requirements and technical levels, by promoting system optimization and software testing throughout the process, and by encouraging the team to regularly review and critique their iterative work for continuous improvement.

In addition to optimizing the software development process, Lean focuses on the critical importance of having a cross-functional project team that is sufficiently skilled, resourced and empowered to deliver the highest-value outcomes to the department.

Kanban

Kanban is an Agile workload and change management methodology that can be used in conjunction with or independently from other Agile methodologies. Currently, it is being used most extensively to manage IT support and maintenance activities, where priority work can change on a weekly, daily or even hourly basis.

At the heart of Kanban is a drive to empower the project team to regularly deliver business value by limiting their work in progress (WIP) at any point in time. This means that the team only commits to work that they can genuinely deliver: no more and no less. If the business requires a higher-priority task to be addressed, stakeholders must determine what current work should be postponed in order to free up sufficient resources to address the requirement. Equally, if the team has an opening in the WIP queue, stakeholders can determine the highest-priority work that the team should focus on next.

Kanban visualizes the workflow through the use of centralized Kanban boards to make the following information evident to all stakeholders at any time:

- The status of all of the project team's planned, current and completed work
- The team's availability to take on additional work
- Any hurdles that are preventing work from progressing.

Not only does this practice create an environment of open communication, transparency and collaboration – it also promotes a culture of continuous improvement by encouraging teams to address bottlenecks, overcome hurdles and maximize their productivity throughout the process.[23]

While Scrum prescribes managing work in time-boxed iterations, and FDD™ prescribes committing to work

Kanban is an Agile methodology for workload and change management that is used to:

• Allow project teams (particularly IT support and maintenance teams) to manage their workload in order to:
  o Ensure regular outputs
  o Accommodate changing requirements
  o Make ongoing work transparent to all stakeholders to encourage communication, collaboration and problem solving.

Kanban can be used in conjunction with other Agile methodologies (e.g. Scrum and Lean) to allow the project team to work closely with stakeholders and to deliver outputs in time-boxed intervals.

by deliverable features, Kanban is far less prescriptive on *how* a body of work is defined and *when* it can be delivered. Instead, Kanban allows the project team to establish review cycles and release timeframes based on the specific requirements of the department. To accommodate this, Agile practitioners have begun using hybrid methodologies,

---

[23] Some organizations choose to manage all of the work across the department on one Kanban board, with colored sticky notes used to distinguish separate initiatives. This enables commitments and resource availability across the department to be viewed more holistically.

such as Scrum-ban (a combination of Scrum and Kanban), to incorporate effective Agile practices, such as daily stand-up meetings, into the responsiveness of Kanban.

It is important to note that Kanban is a methodology for managing what work is being done by the project team, and for allowing the department to *adjust* activities in the WIP queue to address the highest-priority business requirements. Unlike other Agile methodologies, however, Kanban does not prescribe how the project team works with stakeholders to identify and confirm software features; nor does it prescribe how these features are to be tested and integrated into existing software components.

Most importantly, Kanban does not structure work in time-boxed iterations. This may make this Agile approach better suited to IT departments where there is a constant flow of ongoing work, rather than project-based deliverables.

Rational Unified Process® (RUP®)

The Rational Unified Process® (RUP®) is a framework of Agile best-practice approaches that are designed around iterative software development work, and with a strong focus on *identifying and addressing risks* as early in the project as possible. Although the framework is flexible to adapt to the needs of each project, the primary objective of *risk mitigation* is a critical factor in every RUP® implementation.

RUP® work is commonly divided into four phases:

1. Inception: This is when the project scope is identified and confirmed through a business case, a description of the work, an initial (or basic) use case model, budget forecasting, an estimated delivery schedule, and a risk assessment. All aspects of the planned project work are confirmed by key stakeholders prior to progressing to the next phase.

2. **Elaboration:** This is when the team develops the bulk of the use cases (which document the users' interaction with the system) and the system architecture for the solution. The primary focus of this phase is the *identification and mitigation of technical risks* in the solution. This is done by adding in use cases that specifically target identified risks, prototyping risk areas to show that they can be addressed, and by utilizing an *executable architecture* for the most critical use cases. Work within this phase can be done *iteratively*, with the most risky areas being addressed in the initial iterations[24]. Original project estimations are confirmed during this phase, which includes the creation of a detailed development plan for stakeholder confirmation. The Elaboration phase is considered complete when stakeholders are confident that all identified risks have been sufficiently addressed, that the system design is sound, and that the updated project schedule (including budget utilization and resourcing) is sufficiently accurate to proceed.

3. **Construction:** This is when the actual development work is undertaken by the team in support of the approved use cases. The RUP® is not prescriptive about the development platform that teams use, but strongly advocates the use of an object-oriented environment to facilitate the development and integration of discrete use

---

[24] See *Risk reduction with the RUP® phase plan*, Aked M (2003) (*www.ibm.com/developerworks/rational/library/1826.html#N100E4*) for detailed information on using the Elaboration phase to mitigate identified risks.

cases, which then provide a greater opportunity for ongoing quality control and code reuse. Work in the Construction phase is generally done *across multiple iterations*, culminating with an initial operational capability (IOC) review, where stakeholders assess developed capabilities and confirm project readiness for deployment.

4. **Transition:** This is when the approved capabilities are deployed to users with the necessary documentation and training to support the successful use of the solution in a production environment. Depending on the size of the system, work in the Transition phase can also be done *iteratively,* with subsets of capabilities released when the organization is in a position to utilize them. Transition phase work continues until the users are able to utilize – and are satisfied with – all the released capabilities (i.e. the "product release milestone").

A key differentiation between the RUP® and other Agile methodologies (e.g. Scrum) is that, with the RUP®, the iterative work of the Elaboration, Construction and Transition phases is done within the boundaries of the *initial scoping work* that was done in the Inception phase. Accordingly, the RUP® is considered to be an *iterative software development* methodology, instead of an *iterative project delivery* methodology. The result is that the RUP® can be used to mitigate the risks associated with implementing agreed functionality, but is less effective at addressing the risks of internal or external changes to business requirements as project work progresses.

For organizations transitioning from waterfall to Agile approaches in software development, the RUP® can provide a "safer" starting point: one that introduces the project team to the principles and practices of iterative work without dramatically changing the

> The **Rational Unified Process**® **(RUP**®**)** is an iterative software development methodology that focuses on identifying and addressing risks as early in the project as possible.
>
> The RUP® is executed through four phases: *Inception, Elaboration, Construction* and *Transition*. The initial scope and metrics for the project (e.g. timeline, budget) are identified in the Inception phase. Iterative work can be undertaken over the next three phases, but always within the constraints of the initially approved project scope.
>
> Risk management is a critical component of all four phases of the RUP®, with progression to each subsequent phase contingent upon the successful demonstration that identified risks have been sufficiently addressed.

upfront specification approach that they are familiar with. Similarly, for projects that are subject to existing scope constraints (e.g. fixed scope contracts), the RUP® offers a way to introduce *some* of the key benefits of Agile (primarily risk mitigation) within the immovable constraints of a fixed deliverable. It is, however, important to recognize the limitations of the RUP® in delivering all of the benefits identified in *Chapter 3: The Core Business Benefits of Agile*, particularly *responsiveness to business change*.

Essential Unified Process (EssUP)

The Essential Unified Process (EssUP) is an *expansion* of the RUP®. It differs in two significant ways:

1. The EssUP provides a *more extensive range of practices* for teams to use in their development work, in their management of business requirements, and in their overall product delivery. These include practices for establishing scalable technology platforms, for team building and for business process improvement. The EssUP also incorporates a range of Agile practices, such as time-boxed iterations and business-driven use cases.[25]

2. The EssUP provides *more flexibility* than the RUP®, allowing teams to pick and choose the subset of practices that are best suited to the needs of each project, each team, and each organization.

To encourage and facilitate the use of these practices, the EssUP uses "process cards" (also referred to as "playing cards"), which describe the processes for each practice in a structure that is far more accessible to teams than a detailed process manual. Where teams need more information on how to use a specific process in their work, they can also refer to the corresponding guidelines document.

---

[25] See Ivar Jacobson's website (*www.ivarjacobson.com/uploadedFiles/Pages/Knowledge Centre/Resources/Collateral/R esources/EssentialPractices2_Brochure.pdf*) for the full list of essential practices in the EssUP.

The most important distinction between the RUP® and the EssUP is that the EssUP is *not* prescriptive about which practices are used for each project; it is left to the discretion of each project team to determine which EssUP practices can best improve (or supplement) their current work practices.

In this way, the EssUP adapts the more rigid, risk-management-driven

The **Essential Unified Process (EssUP)** expands upon the RUP® by:

- Providing a more extensive range of practices for teams to use
- Providing more flexibility by allowing teams to "pick and choose" the subset of practices that are best suited to their needs.

The EssUP includes practices for scaling technical solutions, for team building and for business process improvement, as well as a range of Agile practices.

structures of the RUP® into a more holistic, Agile-driven approach that represent best practices for overall product life cycle implementation.

Agile Unified Process (AUP)

For organizations that want the discipline of the RUP®, the flexibility of the EssUP, and the benefits of XP practices, the Agile Unified Process (AUP) provides a "best of all worlds" Agile approach.

The AUP works within the Inception, Elaboration, Construction and Transition phases of the RUP®, but simplifies the structure of the RUP® to seven key disciplines: *model, implementation, test, deployment, configuration management, project management* and *environment.* Importantly, the AUP incorporates numerous Agile practices (particularly XP practices) as part of the iterative work *within* the RUP® phases to ensure that development is continually focused on the customer's highest-priority features. To further supplement the risk management features of RUP®, the AUP advocates migrating iterative releases of tested functionality into a *pre-production* environment prior to the full transition of the solution into the live environment.

> The **Agile Unified Process (AUP)** provides a "best of all worlds" Agile approach, particularly for organizations who want the benefits of Agile within a more stringent risk management structure.
>
> Combining the RUP, the EssUP and the best practices of XP, the AUP gives organizations the artifacts that they expect from a traditional software development process, but equally delivers the core benefits of Agile with the iterative delivery of the customer's highest-priority capabilities.

As described by its creator, Scott Ambler, the AUP is "serial in the large" and "iterative in the small"[26].

Like the EssUP, the AUP provides *lightweight documentation*, with teams having the option to refer to more detailed guidelines as needed. Also like the EssUP, the AUP is *adaptable*, so that teams can apply those practices that are best suited to the needs of each project.

To facilitate the adaptation of the developed solution to meet ongoing business requirements, the AUP further

---

[26] The Agile Unified Process (AUP): *www.ambysoft.com/unifiedprocess/agileUP.html.*

encourages teams to use simple tools, scalable architectures and database refactoring.

In many respects, the AUP is the ideal approach for more traditional organizations that are transitioning to Agile methodologies, as it combines both the core principles of Agile and the power of XP practices with the risk management structure of the RUP® and the standard artifacts that organizations expect from a traditional software development process.

Hybrid and emerging Agile methodologies

In describing the range of Agile methodologies above, it was identified that most Agile approaches are designed to deliver efficiencies within a specific area of focus, such as iterative project management or iterative software development. In response to this, many organizations have chosen to implement *hybrid* or *custom* Agile approaches, which leverage the benefits across several different Agile methodologies.

One of the most commonly combined Agile methodologies is Scrum (as an overarching project management approach), which can be used in conjunction with more targeted software development methodologies (e.g. XP or Lean) or workload management methodologies (e.g. Kanban).

There is, however, another interesting trend that is emerging as a result of experienced Agile practitioners wanting to leverage the benefits of Agile, but to *adapt* these approaches to better address their specific constraints. One example is the customized set of Agile approaches developed initially for SunCorp, and now available to the industry through the Agile Academy[27].

---

[27] Agile Academy: *www.agileacademy.com.au/agile/about_us*.

CHAPTER 5: WHO USES AGILE?

As identified in *Chapter 1: What is Agile?*, Agile methodologies are used by thousands of organizations worldwide – including Bankwest, Nokia Siemens Networks, Yahoo!, Google, Microsoft, SunCorp and BT – to produce high business-value outcomes in the delivery of their software solutions. Agile methodologies have been equally successful in private and public sector organizations of all sizes, particularly throughout the United States and Europe.

As an example, one of the most common Agile methodologies, Scrum, is used by a number of diverse organizations worldwide, including Adobe, Barclays Global Investors, the BBC's New Media Division, BellSouth, Bose, Capital One®, GE, Google, Microsoft, Motorola, Nokia Siemens Networks, SAP®, State Farm® and Yahoo![28]

---

[28] The use of Scrum by these organizations is documented in numerous of sources, including corporate websites, industry publications (e.g. *Microsoft Lauds Scrum Method for Software Projects*, Taft DK (2005): *www.eweek.com/c/a/IT-Management/Microsoft-Lauds-Scrum-Method-for-Software-Projects/*), the work undertaken by industry experts such as Jeff Sutherland (*http://scrumtraininginstitute.com/classes/show/85*) and case studies at industry events, such as *The Growth of an Agile Coach Community at a Fortune 200 Company*, Silva K & Doss C, AGILE 2007, Washington DC (August 13th – 17th 2007): *http://ieeexplore.ieee.org/Xplore/login.jsp?url=http%3A%2F%2Fieeexplore.ieee.org%2 Fiel5%2F4293562%2F4293563%2F04293600.pdf%3Farnumber%3D4293600&authDec ision=-203.*

5: Who Uses Agile?

One of the co-founders of Yahoo! said, "Agile has been one of the most positive things to happen to the company"[29].

Forrester's September 2006 survey of technology decision makers[30] identified that 17% of North American and European businesses use Agile methodologies, while another 29% are aware of them. A more recent survey undertaken by VersionOne[31] indicates that organizations that use Agile in their software delivery are achieving increased productivity (74% of respondents), faster time to completion (66% of respondents) and improved ability to manage changes in requirements (87% of respondents).

This track record can give readers confidence in knowing that Agile methodologies are sustainable, proven approaches that are successfully used throughout the global marketplace.

---

[29] http://campustechnology.com/articles/2008/02/lessons-from-a-yahoo-scrum-rollout.aspx
Further detail on Yahoo!'s use of Agile practices is also provided in *Rolling out Agile in a Large Enterprise*, Benefield G (2008):
www.computer.org/portal/web/csdl/doi/10.1109/HICSS.2008.382.
[30] *The state of application development in enterprises and SMBs: business data services North America and Europe*, Stone J, Database & Network Journal (Apr 1st 2007):
www.thefreelibrary.com/_/print/PrintArticle.aspx?id=162832944.
[31] 2010 State of Agile Development survey results:
www.versionone.com/pdf/2010_State_of_Agile_Development_Survey_Results.pdf.

CHAPTER 6: WHY DON'T MORE ORGANIZATIONS USE AGILE?

As identified in the previous chapter, there are numerous organizations worldwide that have used – and that continue to use – Agile approaches to successfully deliver their IT outcomes. Despite their strong and vocal support of Agile approaches, however, there are still some hurdles in the more widespread adoption of Agile in the broader IT community. These include:

Lack of awareness

Over the past two decades, the Agile community has grown from a handful of passionate advocates to a worldwide presence in thousands of organizations. There are numerous books, websites, industry forums, conferences and training courses dedicated to the establishment, management and refinement of Agile approaches (*Chapter 21: More Information on Agile* provides details on several of these resources). The people who actively use Agile approaches in their work are generally staunch supporters of their benefits, but they also tend to communicate more within their own circles than with the IT community at large.

In the past several years, prominent industry research organizations, such as Forrester[32], have published reports documenting the use of Agile approaches in the industry,

---

[32] *The state of application development in enterprises and SMBs: business data services North America and Europe*, Stone J, Database & Network Journal (Apr 1st 2007): www.thefreelibrary.com/ /print/PrintArticle.aspx?id=162832944.

which include the benefits that organizations who adopt these approaches are achieving. There have also been a handful of articles on Agile approaches in prominent IT industry publications, such as *CIO Magazine*[33]. These publications, combined with Agile success stories from notable organizations, indicate that it is reasonable to expect that awareness of Agile in the IT industry will increase over time; however, the education process is more of a slow progression than a giant leap.

The fact that you are reading this book puts you several steps ahead of others in the industry who are unaware of Agile, or who may have been discouraged by misinformation about these approaches (*see Agile myths below for further detail*). Being aware of Agile approaches is the first step; fitting Agile work within the culture and constraints of your organization is the real hurdle to overcome.

The "Business as usual" mindset

In many respects, Agile approaches make a significant (some might even say radical) departure from the traditional approaches used by organizations to deliver IT solutions – particularly waterfall methods. The traditional approaches, despite their pitfalls (*see Chapter 2: A Five Minute History of Agile*), provide organizations with the upfront planning, heavy documentation, and highly

---

[33] *Agile Programming 101: An Executive Guide to Agile Programming* (2008): www.cio.com.au/article/268197/agile_programming_101_an_executive_guide_agile_pro gramming/?fp=4&fpid=23 and *Getting Clueful: 7 Things CIOs Should Know About Agile Development*, Schindler E (2008): www.cio.com/article/180402/Getting_Clueful_7_Things_CIOs_Should_Know_About_Agi le_Development?page=1.

supervised environment that managers are familiar with. In some cases, these organizations are so embedded in the comfort zone of traditional approaches that they cannot objectively see the direct correlation between these approaches and the budget overruns and missed deadlines (or complete failure) of their IT initiatives.

Agile approaches do require IT departments to act – and think – differently from the way that they have in the past. IT directors who are self-aware (and humble) enough to recognize that their business practices of the past may not sustain them into the future, will be more amenable to considering Agile – especially given the widespread support and long history of success of its approaches. In contrast, IT directors who are committed to "the way we do things around here" are likely to see Agile approaches as too radical for their organization. The bottom line is that Agile approaches require that significant changes be made to the way in which IT departments operate – but change can be for the *better*.

"Agile does not fit within our organization"

This is, arguably, one of the most common concerns expressed by IT directors when it comes to adopting Agile approaches. They have read a myriad of Agile success stories, they appreciate how much these approaches could dramatically improve the work in their department, but they are concerned that Agile approaches will be seen as too radical (or risky) by the organization. Even those IT directors who are in a position to implement Agile methodologies are unsure of how approaches advocating incremental and iterative work will fit within the annual budgeting, upfront project planning and corporate reporting mandates within their organization.

As alignment with the organization is a crucial component of successful widespread Agile adoption, several sections of this book have been written to address these specific management concerns – starting with *Chapter 12: Aligning Agile with Your Corporate Culture*. Subsequent chapters address how to incorporate Agile work within a range of management activities – from staffing to corporate reporting to managing departmental budgets.

Agile myths

In a world where anyone can voice their opinions (substantiated or otherwise) on blogs, social media sites, and industry forums, a little knowledge is definitely a dangerous thing.

Because Agile approaches *are* substantially different from traditional IT approaches, it is natural for people in the industry who are relatively unfamiliar with Agile to latch onto those aspects of it that seem to be the greatest departure from their normal work practices; and to exaggerate these differences. Exaggerations of Agile approaches are rarely malicious; they are more likely to be based on a misunderstanding of – or a lack of direct experience in – the use of the approaches. Some of the most common Agile myths include:

"Agile work does not require planning": It is true that Agile approaches discourage the creation of large upfront plans that try to predict everything that might happen over the course of a project. Instead, the Agile approach is to use *incremental planning* throughout the project, which

includes the regular review, confirmation and adjustment of plans at each iteration to reflect the most current information available to the team.

"Agile work does not require documentation": Although Agile approaches do encourage the use of active face-to-face communication as the most effective method for exchanging information, Agile work *fully supports* the development of documentation to the extent that is appropriate for the organization. This includes:

- Documenting business rules and other supporting details to clarify user requirements
- Producing documentation to meet organizational compliance requirements, such as PRINCE2® stage plans
- Documenting system behavior to support ongoing training, administration and recordkeeping requirements. (It should be noted that system documentation for Agile work is often produced retrospectively during – or even after – the release of the system. This not only allows the project team to focus on their core work during the development process, but also results in documentation that is often more cost-effective to produce – e.g. by using screen captures from the delivered solution, which also tends to better reflect the actual behavior of the released system.)

"Agile projects are unmanaged": Agile methodologies encourage a different form of management from that that traditional organizations may be used to. Instead of top-down mandates and closely monitored staff, project teams are empowered to do the work that is required under the guidance and oversight of stakeholders. This results in the

establishment of self-organized teams. Management is able to oversee the productivity and value of each project team's work through Agile measuring and monitoring tools, such as executive dashboards, product backlogs and Kanban boards (as described in *Chapter 10: Using Agile Tools*). Arguably, however, the most definitive method of oversight is reviewing the team's ongoing production of tangible, high business-value outputs that are presented at the end of each time-boxed iteration.

Historical misapplication

This chapter has, so far, focused on the hurdles that can prevent IT departments from initially pursuing Agile approaches to overcome the inefficiencies in their work. But what if your department *has* used Agile approaches in the past, only to find that they did not generate the same successful results as in other organizations? Although Agile may not be the best fit for every organization, in many cases, unsuccessful attempts at implementing Agile approaches are actually the result of the *misapplication* of these approaches.

One of the most common areas of misapplication occurs when organizations implement Agile approaches in a way that *undermines* the underlying principles. This could be, for example, an organization that moves to an "Agile" iteration-based project management model, but still requires all of the work to be signed-off in an upfront specification. Truly Agile organizations understand that incremental planning is only valuable when the organization is in a position to *adapt* ongoing work as it progresses. Otherwise, iterative work just becomes shorter delivery cycles that are limited by the same core constraint; and Agile approaches get an unjustified bad reputation when this pre-constrained process inevitably fails.

Similarly, there are organizations who have implemented selected Agile practices (such as Test-Driven Development) within their IT department, but who have not actively involved the customer in the ongoing review and adjustment of their work. Although the adoption of Agile practices within the IT department is likely to produce higher-quality software (i.e. fewer bugs), the lack of involvement from the business areas who will be using the developed software means that the department has not confirmed that the delivered software genuinely meets the needs of the business. Equally, this means that the department has not mitigated the risk of developers spending their time building low-value software features that are rarely (if ever) used. The active involvement of the customers who require the software is a critical component of ensuring that the development work done by your staff is consistently focused on delivering the most relevant and valuable software features.

Last, there are practices in the software industry that have elements of Agile (and are therefore referred to as "Agile" by their practitioners), but which lack some of the fundamental features of Agile methodologies for them to truly be considered in this category. One example of this is "spiral methodology" development work, where the customer is presented with *functional prototypes* of system capabilities throughout the development process in order to confirm intended system behavior. Although the spiral methodology approach is a valid way to engage the customer and to confirm system design, it *does not* deliver fully functional, fully tested, production-ready software as part of these customer reviews. This means that most of the *ongoing risk management* (for technical risk) and *delivery of tangible outputs* benefits of true Agile approaches are not available to the organization with methodologies such as these.

Chapter 8: Delivering Agile provides guidance on how to "sell" the *proper use* of Agile to decision makers in the organization, including those people who mistakenly think that "iterative waterfall", "development in isolation of the customer", "spiral methodology" and other misguided variations on Agile are able to deliver the advantages identified in *Chapter 3: The Core Business Benefits of Agile.*

CHAPTER 7: IS AGILE RIGHT FOR MY DEPARTMENT?

The previous chapters provided you with information on the benefits that implementing Agile could provide to your department, described a range of Agile approaches that organizations use, and identified the prevalence of Agile approaches in organizations worldwide. All of this information is intended to give you the background knowledge to make an informed decision as to whether Agile approaches are a good match for the specific needs of your department.

Although the low overhead of implementing Agile methodologies may make it tempting for your department to dive right in and start using these approaches, it would be a good idea to step back for a moment and consider whether Agile is truly suited to your department. To do this, you need to ask yourself the following six critical questions:

Question one: What are the biggest challenges in my department?

Is your department under pressure to achieve difficult deadlines? Are there too few people to get the work done, or insufficient budget allocations? Or are you facing a combination of all of these factors?

Are staff not as productive as they could (or should) be? Are the business processes, equipment or communication channels that they use slowing them down? Is there too much corporate knowledge in the heads of a handful of employees? Or are low-quality outputs creating the need for constant "fire-fighting" and damage control?

Every IT department can benefit to some degree by using Agile approaches, but those departments that have the most significant issues also have the most to gain from the Agile approaches that specifically target these issues. This is why Agile approaches are ideally suited to departments where there are ongoing issues with:

* The quality of delivered solutions
* Delivering software solutions within agreed timelines and/or budgets
* Delivered solutions adequately supporting business requirements
* High staff turnover rates (or low staff productivity levels).

The level of benefit that your department is likely to receive from implementing Agile methodologies is also directly correlated with the following risk factors:

* The potential for requirements to change *while* the solution is being developed, including:
  o *Internal changes*: changes in user requirements, staff departures, business priority shifts, funding reallocations
  o *External changes:* changes in customer requirements, fluctuations in market demand, announcements from competitors, the availability of new technologies.
* The sustainability of your current IT overheads, including costs of development, implementation, maintenance and support.

If your software solutions are based on *highly predictable* and *replicable* business processes with a minimal likelihood of changing requirements, then your department will not achieve the same level of benefit from Agile as one that is more susceptible to solution requirements that are likely to change over time.

The same is true for departments where current software solutions are delivered on time, align well with business requirements and require minimal ongoing support to address quality and usability issues.

In each of these situations, Agile methodologies can provide some degree of benefit to the department, but not the dramatic benefits that departments with more dynamic (and less sustainable) software solutions can achieve.

The bottom line is that the more your department is faced with changing requirements and/or unsustainable IT overheads, the better positioned you are to receive substantial returns on your Agile investment.

Question two: Am I looking for a "quick fix" solution?

Implementing Agile methodologies in your department will not change your budget expenditure from red to black in a matter of weeks, or even months. Time is needed for staff to become familiar with these approaches, to refine their use of Agile to align with the specific requirements of your department, and to organically grow the use of Agile to a sufficiently critical mass of IT projects that can offset the losses from traditionally-managed software projects.

This means that the introduction of Agile methodologies is not likely to result in a substantial decrease in software development costs in your department. In fact, during the initial implementation of these approaches, there are likely to be additional overheads associated with training and knowledge sharing, establishing supporting technologies (e.g. automated testing environments), and establishing centralized locations for project teams to work and collaborate in.

Agile methodologies are far more likely to result in *longer-term cost savings* for your department by delivering software solutions that are of a significantly higher quality, have far greater usability, and are much more aligned to the highest-priority business needs of the organization.

Therefore, the most relevant ROI calculation for your organization is *not* likely to be a side-by-side comparison of *software development costs* for projects using traditional processes versus Agile methodologies; it will be a side-by-side comparison of the *whole-of-life costs* of developing, maintaining, supporting and extending each of these software solutions, and will include tracking turnover rates for both IT staff and (where appropriate) the business areas utilizing these solutions.

Think of Agile as an investment in your department's IT future, particularly in reducing the whole-of-life costs of maintaining, supporting and extending the software solutions that your staff deliver.

Question three: Are the people in my department prepared to change their "business as usual" routines?

For some organizations – particularly larger and older ones – the answer to this question is likely to be "no". The idea of implementing methodologies that:

- Encourage the *evolution* of business requirements, instead of relying upon upfront signed-off documentation
- Empower the project team to *self-organize*, instead of controlling their daily activities, and
- Replace reams of documentation with *face-to-face communication*

may seem a bit daunting for some staff – particularly for those who have grown comfortable in their day-to-day routines (even comfortable with the project issues and last-minute "firefighting" that can result from their "business as usual" work).

If your staff are a bit hesitant at first, you may find that trialing an Agile project in your department will be sufficient to get them familiar with – and motivated by – these approaches. *See Chapter 8: Delivering Agile for guidelines on selecting the right trial project.*

If, however, after trialing one or two Agile projects, staff are still uncomfortable working directly with the business areas, supporting changing requirements as the project progresses, and self-managing their work, it may be that Agile approaches are just not suited to your organizational culture. Or you may need to seriously consider staff changes, as discussed in *Chapter 17: Building the Right Agile Team.*

Question four: Are your executives prepared for your department to use Agile approaches?

Agile can be seen by executives as a radical departure from traditional software delivery methods. Those who *have heard* about Agile approaches may have also been exposed to some of the Agile myths identified in *Chapter 6: Why Don't More Organizations Use Agile?* Also, some of the terms used ("eXtreme Programming™", for example) can create the impression that these are "rogue" practices instead of proven approaches.

Chapter 5: Who Uses Agile? identified a number of highly reputable organizations worldwide that use Agile methodologies, including several (e.g. Microsoft and Yahoo!) that have published case studies documenting the benefits of these approaches. These are not rogue start-up organizations with radical notions of success; they are organizations with structured key performance indicators (KPIs), bottom-line imperatives and accountability to shareholders. If Agile methodologies are able to deliver significant business-value benefits to these organizations, it is reasonable for executives to expect comparable returns in your department.

Question five: Are *you* prepared for Agile?

At the heart of Agile approaches is the firm belief that people can – and will – do the right thing by the organization if they are given the opportunity.

In order for Agile approaches to work, directors and managers who have traditionally maintained heavy-handed control over the day-to-day work of their staff will need to be willing to relinquish that control in favor of *trusting* and *empowering* their staff.

The structure of Agile methodologies means that management does not need to keep a close watch on every step that the project team makes, because they know that they are never more than a few weeks away from seeing the tangible results of their work. This means that management can be confident that work is progressing without having to constantly monitor staff, and staff are entrusted, empowered and left alone to do the work that they have committed to. There are, however, a number of *additional benefits* to empowering the staff in your department, as self-organized teams are ideally positioned to provide the department with:

* Specialist, hands-on knowledge of the actual work required
* Natural skills and strengths compensation
* More realistic estimates of the work that can be achieved
* Motivation for the team to *want to* achieve the work that they have actively committed to.

Another interesting thing about the dynamic of self-organizing teams is that, as they progress, they are able to create *ongoing motivation* for employees. Project team members know that their continued ability to self-manage their work depends on their regular delivery of high-value business outcomes. Additionally, because they are the ones who identify what work can (and cannot) be achieved in each iteration, they are motivated by their personal responsibility to achieve these outcomes. This combination of factors is heightened by the satisfaction and pride that staff members feel when they produce tangible outputs that truly meet the needs of the organization.

As an IT director, the power rests in your hands to promote this shift in management style, and to strategically select the right project managers when introducing Agile approaches to the department.

Question six: Are the intended participants sufficiently aware of Agile principles and practices?

In *Chapter 6: Why Don't More Organizations Use Agile?*, it was identified that one of the biggest hurdles to the successful adoption of Agile approaches in an organization is the historical misapplication of these approaches as *techniques* not principles. It is not enough for the people who participate in Agile work to understand the *mechanisms* of these activities; they also need to understand the *intent* in order for them to most effectively utilize these approaches.

In the example that was provided, the misapplication of Agile approaches related to organizations using iteration-based project planning against a *predefined upfront specification*, which only served to provide them with more frequently delivered misaligned outcomes.

This is why it is essential that each team member understands the principles that underpin Agile work. *Chapter 8: Delivering Agile* includes information on the best ways to educate participants about the intent and mechanisms of Agile approaches, including the importance of their roles.

If the information provided in this chapter has given you the assurance – and the motivation – to pursue Agile approaches within your department, the remaining sections of this book can provide you with the strategies, tactics and resources needed to realistically achieve this goal within the structure (and the constraints) of your organization.

CHAPTER 8: DELIVERING AGILE

There is no one formula for successfully introducing Agile approaches within an IT department. Historically, some organizations have preferred to start by trialing Agile approaches on a small set of projects – in order to see how effective they are – and then expand their use of Agile approaches as staff became more comfortable with Agile practices, such as incremental planning or working directly with the customer. Decision makers in a handful of organizations, including the forward-thinking senior executive of BT[34], have jump-started the adoption process by instituting a top-down mandate for using Agile approaches across the IT department, with the directive for all staff to deliver high business-value outcomes every 90 days. (This is, however, a noted exception case.)[35]

It is far more likely that the adoption of Agile methodologies in your department will need to begin with using these approaches on a few small projects, tracking the outcomes, and then using their success to motivate other project teams to do the same. The following section, *Choosing the right kick-off point*, provides some guidelines for you to follow in determining the best projects to use as your starting point.

---

[34] *Agile Coaching in British Telecom*, Meadows L and Hanly S (2006): www.agilejournal.com/articles/columns/column-articles/144-agile-coaching-in-british-telecom.

[35] Even if you are in a position to influence the adoption of Agile approaches across your department, you may still want to begin with a few selected initiatives. This will allow staff to get used to the structure and dynamic of Agile approaches – and be motivated by their effectiveness – before the approaches are more broadly applied.

Choosing the right kick-off point

Deciding where to begin using Agile methodologies in your department is as important as deciding which methodology you will use.

Is your objective to do a "safe" trial of Agile before committing to its broader use across the department? If so, you may want to select a self-contained new software development project that will not be unduly burdened by the constraints of legacy systems or pre-existing project management techniques.

Is your objective to create some "runs on the board" to influence others to consider using Agile methodologies? If so, then you need to choose projects that are important enough, so that their success will be meaningful to the organization. Achieving great results on trivial projects will only serve to fuel resistance from others who may believe that Agile approaches are not applicable to their projects.

Is your objective to use Agile approaches to begin to shift the department towards a more open and collaborative working environment? If so, you may want to start with the path of least cultural resistance by choosing a particular project team that is most likely to be amenable to working closely with business areas, trusting and empowering team members, and measuring success through the production and demonstration of tangible results.

Once you have selected the project(s) that align with your core objectives, the next step is to determine which Agile methodologies and practices are best suited to the needs of the selected project(s).

Choosing the right methodologies and practices

Agile methodologies are not a "one size fits all" proposition. For these methodologies to deliver genuine business value to your department, it is important to find the right Agile methodology (or combination of methodologies and practices) to address your specific department's challenges, your KPIs and your culture. It is equally important to *work with the selected project teams* in making this decision.

Chapter 9: Selecting the Right Agile Approach for Your Needs provides an Agile methodologies selection workflow tool that takes you through some of the key questions that you need to ask in order to select the most appropriate Agile methodologies and practices for each of your selected projects.

Creating a shared understanding of Agile

As indicated in the previous chapter, the only way for Agile work to be successful in your department is if the people who participate are aware of both the *intent* and the *mechanisms* of using the approaches. If they *aren't*, the potential for the Agile approaches to be misapplied will be significantly increased, which could eliminate the possibility of wider organizational support altogether (*see Chapter 6: Why Don't More Organizations Use Agile?*)

Before you begin using Agile in your department, you should consider how the basics of these approaches are going to be disseminated to the people who will be involved in the process.

For some organizations, the best way to educate staff is to empower them to learn about the processes themselves –

through online resources and books, such as those listed in *Chapter 21: More Information on Agile*. Your corporate intranet can include an Agile resources page that provides links to relevant sites and allows the people in the department to exchange their questions, concerns and ideas about the use of the approaches before work begins

For other organizations, sharing of information may be best achieved by creating an easy-to-use guide that explains the basics of Agile approaches in the context of your organizational culture (such as the "Agile Cookbook" that was created by BT), and then supplementing these guides with internal training sessions to walk through and demonstrate these approaches.

Alternatively, you may want to educate a small group of staff members about using Agile approaches for one initiative, and then document the outcomes of their work as a case study to bring to other project teams.

Whichever way you decide to share this information, it is critical that participants understand both the approaches and their respective roles. It is equally important that they appreciate the returns that they are likely to receive from their participation – which include empowered teams, higher-quality outputs and less "fire-fighting" to meet their deadlines – so that they will be motivated to get started.

Aligning Agile work with your traditional projects

Unless you are mandating the use of Agile approaches across the department, your staff will most likely be working on a combination of Agile projects and projects that use traditional methods (most commonly waterfall approaches). The ideal model is to keep these projects completely separate – allowing the Agile project work to use incremental planning, so that the resulting solutions can evolve with the customer's requirements. However, it may not always be possible to separate work – or staff – into these two distinct camps.

If you are trying to salvage an existing waterfall project by moving the work to use Agile approaches instead, *Chapter 16: Establishing Agile Contracts* provides a number of guidelines for dealing with pre-existing scope, time and budget constraints in project work.

If you are trying to get a waterfall project team to work jointly with an Agile project team (e.g. integrating two related systems), then *ongoing communication* between the teams is critical. Each project team will need to be fully aware of the status of the other team's work, requiring regular updates on outputs produced and issues encountered. This will enable the work being undertaken by the waterfall project team (including any fixed capabilities or deadlines) to be treated as *external constraints* by the Agile project team, which can then be factored into the prioritization of ongoing work. Ideally, the joint work between the teams will also involve a business (or management) representative who has authority to make priority decisions when there is a conflict between the projects (e.g. a fixed capability in the waterfall project that contradicts an emerging requirement in the Agile project, or a limitation in available resources across both projects).

Preferably, exposure to the use of Agile approaches will be so compelling to the waterfall project team that they will take action to use Agile methodologies – or even to trial selected Agile practices – in subsequent phases of their work.

Conquering the tyranny of distance

Ongoing communication is one of the most critical components in the successful delivery of Agile projects – both with the customer and within the team itself. *Chapter 4: Common Agile Methodologies at a Glance* described a number of Agile approaches where high communication (and even the *co-location* of team members) was an essential part of the methodology. So what do you do when you have staff (and/or customers) located on different floors, in different office buildings, or even in different countries?

Although Agile approaches advocate the use of *face-to-face communication* wherever possible, Agile practitioners are also realistic about not always having this luxury in a global marketplace. This does *not* mean, however, that staff should resort to the use of documentation in lieu of direct communication.

Where possible, teams should try to use the *closest thing to face-to-face communication* that is available, including:

- Video-conferencing
- Doing paired work via remote desktops
- Using virtual presence tools (such as chat rooms and web-based presentation tools).

Time differences and other constraints may not make constant communication a possibility, but the aim should be to arrange direct communication wherever possible. Ideally, there will also be opportunities for the teams to travel, so that they can work face-to-face at selected times during the course of the project (particularly for iteration planning work and reviews with the customer).

It is important to note that the equivalent advice for effective communication applies to *any* project work where team members are divided, including when the team is working with partners in other organizations and outsourced developers.

The critical component to conquering the tyranny of distance is *not* replacing direct discussion between team members (or with the customer) with the use of documentation. Even virtual face-to-face communication is preferred to the one-sided interpretation of a detailed requirements specification or extensive back-and-forth e-mails.

You might be surprised ...

In introducing Agile approaches within your department, you may, in fact, be surprised to learn that there are project teams within your department who are *already using* Agile practices in their work.

It is quite common for Agile approaches to have been introduced to an IT department by the project team members themselves, often without the active awareness or support of management (otherwise known as "Agile by stealth").

"Agile by stealth" is a subtle way of introducing Agile approaches to an organization from the ground up. Because Agile concepts have tended to be written for a more technical audience, Agile work in the IT industry has traditionally been promoted through "bottom-up" channels – i.e. software developers introduce these approaches to their team leaders, who then present them to management.

Generally this involves project teams using selected Agile practices *informally*, for example:

- Making arrangements with one or more users to work with the team on a deliverable as an "unofficial" customer
- Establishing high-communication channels within the team, such as face-to-face meetings (instead of numerous back-and-forth e-mails) and daily stand-up meetings to check in with each other where possible
- Pairing up with co-workers on the work that they are doing, so that they can each review and critique the other's work while it is progressing
- Doing work in self-imposed time-boxed iterations to ensure that the team is regularly producing valuable outputs.

This "Agile by stealth" approach is generally not the team's preferred way of introducing Agile within the department; they would much rather have your support and backing for this work. Instead, the "Agile by stealth" approach is likely to be perceived by the project team members as a necessary way to ensure that they can progress with these practices "under the radar", without provoking management resistance or challenging the traditional approaches of the department.

If, in your discussions with your staff, you find that they have already been utilizing these methodologies, you are likely to be one step ahead of the game. In most cases, these teams will not have definitive metrics for the work that they have done to date. They are, however, likely to have a number of work products, including delivered software and customer testimonials, which can indicate how well their employed Agile approaches worked. They are also likely to have acquired a substantial amount of knowledge about what does – and does not – work within your organizational culture. All of this information can be applied to selecting the best ongoing approaches for your department to use and the expansion of the project team's Agile work – now with the benefit of your support.

CHAPTER 9: SELECTING THE RIGHT AGILE APPROACH FOR YOUR NEEDS

If you have determined that the nature of your department is reasonably suited to Agile approaches[36] – and you have identified the projects where you want to begin using Agile approaches – then the next challenge is in deciding *which* of these approaches is best suited to the specific demands of your selected projects.

Chapter 4: Common Agile Methodologies at a Glance identified a number of Agile methodologies that have been successfully used in the IT industry over the past 20 years. Some of these approaches are used more commonly than others, most notably Scrum and XP (individually or combined). However, these approaches are more suited to project-based software development activities, and may only be suitable for a subset of the IT work in your department.

The Agile methodologies selection workflow tool in *Figure 1* takes you through some of the key questions that you need to ask in order to select the most appropriate Agile methodologies for each area of work in your department.

---

[36] Or that you are reasonably able to change the current climate to allow these approaches to be successfully introduced.

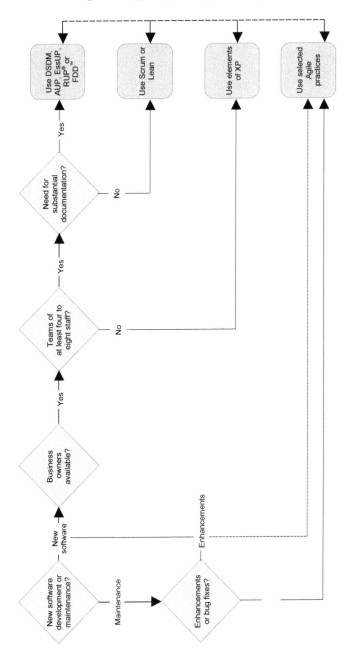

Figure 1: Agile methodologies selection workflow tool

To use the Agile methodologies selection workflow tool, start with the question in the upper left-hand corner:

New software development or maintenance?

- If the project that you have selected is a new software development, then go to the *business owners available?* question below.

- If the project is predominantly a maintenance activity, then the next question to consider is whether or not the maintenance work will include the development of *enhancements or bug fixes?*

- If the project is a maintenance activity for bug fixes, you may be best off starting with Kanban to manage this work.

- If the project is a maintenance activity that includes enhancements, you may decide to treat the enhancements as new software development; in which case, you will want to go to the *stakeholders available?* question in the following section.

Business owners available?

Almost every aspect of Agile methodologies requires involvement from the stakeholders (e.g. customers) who will be using the delivered software. If these stakeholders are unavailable (and your department is not in a position to make them available, or to organize for other resources who can adequately represent their interests), then your options for using Agile methodologies could be extremely limited. Therefore, if the answer to the *business owners available?* question is *no*, then the project team may be able to utilize some selected Agile practices – such as daily stand-up meetings, pair programming or Test-Driven Development – to enhance the quality of their development work. In this way, however, the substantial benefits of using Agile methodologies to deliver usable software solutions that directly align to customer needs may not be achieved.

Teams of at least four to eight staff?

Although this is not a hard-and-fast rule, it is generally believed that the ideal team size for Agile methodologies – such as Scrum – is four to eight team members. If you have fewer than four members on your project team for the selected project, it may be better for your department to consider using elements of XP (noting that at least two team members will be required for pair programming). If you have more than eight team members, it may be better for you to break down the teams into groups of four to eight, and then scale the project work within the selected Agile methodologies.

Need for substantial documentation?

The final question to ask yourself is whether or not the organization (and you personally) prefer for the work undertaken by project teams to be substantially documented throughout the process. If so, it may be better for you to use Agile methodologies, such as DSDM, RUP®, AUP or FDD™, which mandate the generation of work products – such as requirements specifications and domain models – as part of the process. Otherwise, it may be better for you to start with methodologies, such as Scrum or Lean – which are more flexible – to accommodate each project team's preferred work practices.

An additional note regarding the Agile methodologies selection workflow tool: On the right-hand side of the diagram is a series of dotted lines connecting each of the suggested Agile methodologies to the others. These dotted lines indicate that your department may opt to combine selected Agile methodologies – e.g. Scrum and XP, or Lean and Kanban – in order to receive the cumulative benefits available from each approach.

Also, if you have selected more than one area of work as your starting point, it may be valuable for you to trial two or three different Agile methodologies at the same time to see which is the best fit for your department.

It is important to note that the Agile methodologies selection workflow tool is only a guideline for you to use as a starting point in selecting the methodologies and practices that *may be* suited to the unique requirements of your department. Your ongoing use of these approaches is the definitive indicator of how well they meet your needs.

Now that you have determined which Agile approaches are likely to be best suited to your selected projects, the next challenge is in using Agile tools to *monitor* and *measure* this work within your department.

CHAPTER 10: USING AGILE TOOLS[37]

For many organizations, status reporting is an *en masse* activity, generally allocated to time-based increments where employees stop what they are doing in order to provide management with a snapshot of their work progress (e.g. monthly status updates). This monthly reporting cycle is intended to provide frequent enough updates to keep management aware of the status of the work in their area – but without overloading the team with reporting activities (or the manager with paperwork to review). It creates a paper productivity trail where managers take action based on the *appearance* of productivity provided in these reports – and employees can continue focusing on their real work for the next 30 days.

In the Agile world, status reporting is an *ongoing* activity. The same environment that enables project teams to be self-managed also creates an obligation for the project team members to keep others in the department aware of the status of the work that they are doing. This obligation is not just for their management; it is equally important to keep the customer aware of the project team's progress – and, more than anything, it is a tool for the project team to manage itself.

The Agile world has found that the best way to incorporate status reporting in project team work is to allow teams to use the *same tools* to manage and track their own day-to-

---

[37] The information on Agile tools has been adapted from *Agile Productivity Unleashed: Proven Approaches for Achieving Real Productivity Gains in Any Organization*, Jamie Lynn Cooke, IT Governance Publishing (2010).

day work as other stakeholders (e.g. managers and the customer) use to oversee their progress. This means that reporting does not need to be an added step in the project team's work; tracking the progress of their activities is an inherent part of their daily routine.

It is important to emphasize that progress reporting on Agile activities is not the daily tracking of hours in a timesheet. Agile approaches are far less focused on what time has elapsed, and far more focused on what *actual business value* has been produced. That is why the Agile world uses tools that track the progress of work completed and effort remaining to achieve the agreed objectives.

The four tools that are most commonly used in Agile approaches are:

* Requirements backlogs
* Delivery backlogs
* Burndown charts
* Executive dashboards.[38]

The requirements backlog: The requirements backlog is a tool where customers can record and prioritize their business requirements for each iteration, and where the project teams can record the progress of their work during each iteration against these requirements.

---

[38] The Agile reporting tools described in this section are primarily based on the tools used in the Scrum methodology, such as product backlogs and sprint backlogs. However, these have deliberately been changed to more generic names, so that readers can see the potential of using these tools for other Agile approaches beyond Scrum.

The delivery backlog: The delivery backlog is a tool used by the project team to track the details of their day-to-day work for each iteration. This includes breaking down each business requirement/activity into *specific tasks* that the project team members need to complete for that requirement to be met.

The executive dashboard: Executive dashboards are used to summarize the progress within (and across) Agile teams against their stated objectives. These tools provide management with an "at-a-glance" view of the key metrics that the department requires to monitor productivity levels (and business value generation) across the organization.

Burndown charts: Burndown charts are visual tools within the requirements backlog, the delivery backlog and the executive dashboard that enable Agile teams to track their rate of productivity (their "velocity") for the current iteration. Based on this information, they can then self-manage their ongoing productivity levels and estimate the amount of work that they can reasonably achieve in future iterations.

Each of these tools is described in further detail later in this chapter.

Backlogs, burndown charts and executive dashboards are valuable tools for monitoring the progress of the work that is undertaken by the project teams – particularly for day-to-day status tracking. Most important, however, is the progress reporting that is done as part of the iterative review session at the end of each iteration.

Where a monthly paper report describes completed (and pending) work using text, bar charts and graphs, the iterative review session at the end of each iteration provides the customers with *hands-on outputs* in an interactive discussion forum. Unlike the graphs and charts in a monthly report – which can be handcrafted to portray work in the best possible light – iterative review sessions put the work under the microscope, leaving little opportunity for the project team to embellish their accomplishments.

With the iterative review sessions, issues that are impacting organizational productivity are no longer resigned to be red text on page three of a paper report; they are addressed (and ideally resolved) *hands-on* with key decision makers. This makes the iterative review session a much more valuable and meaningful source of progress information for the department than any two-dimensional report (including the Agile tracking tools) can provide. The project team is positioned to get direct feedback on their work from the customer, and the department is positioned to get ongoing value from the project team from the minute that the iterative review session is completed.

Measuring productivity by outputs

If productivity is the measurement of how much business value the project team brings to the organization, then status reporting for Agile work needs to be able to track how much *business value* the project team has produced in each iteration, and when additional business value is anticipated to be delivered.

Agile approaches initially use expected business-value measurements as part of the iteration planning sessions in order to determine:

• The work that should be undertaken by the project team

- The order in which work should be completed (i.e. the top-down priority order in the requirements backlog).

Making an expected business-value calculation is one of the ways to assess the value that each feature represents within the overall initiative. Conversely, the progress (and the corresponding business value) of the overall initiative can be determined by measuring the progress of each of the completed (and remaining) features within that initiative.

For example, if the business value of a new product that the organization is launching is projected to be $3.2 million – and the website for that product is expected to generate 75% of that revenue ($2.4 million) – then the work required to deliver that website can be tracked as a percentage of the overall business value of each requirement being delivered:

- Building the website structure = 40% of the business value ($960,000)
- Creating an e-commerce capability to process orders = 30% of the business value ($720,000)
- Providing an interactive service that allows website users to customize the product to their requirements = 20% of the business value ($480,000)
- Building additional features to make the website more usable (e.g. a reusable customer profile) = 10% of the business value ($240,000).

These metrics allow the department to use Agile tools, such as executive dashboards, to track how much *business value* has been delivered – and how much is remaining – based on the amount of work completed for each of the features at the end of each iteration.

Using the above example, at the end of the second iteration the project team advises that they have completed building the website structure (100%) and have also completed one fifth of the e-commerce capability (20%). Based on this status update, the customer now knows that they have received approximately $1.1 million worth of business value from the completed work[39], and that $1.3 million worth of business value is vested in the remaining work.

It should be noted that the above example is a simplification of the actual business-value calculations required in Agile approaches. The simplified model is intended to highlight the underlying difference between Agile tools and standard corporate reports. There are two areas in particular where the real-world application of Agile approaches is more complex than the example provided:

- The features listed in the bullet points above are too broad to be considered valid Agile user requirements.
- The correlation between a partially completed requirement and its relative business value is subject to the nature of the work, e.g. a half-completed website may (or may not) be releasable in its current form. Therefore, the department may prefer to calculate earned business value only on *completed* requirements.

Departments need to use discretion when applying these calculations to ensure that the expected business value is not significantly over- or under-estimated – or misinterpreted by people who are less familiar with Agile approaches.

---

[39] Based on 100% of $960,000 plus 20% of $720,000 ($144,000).

Tracking overall progress in the requirements backlog

The requirements backlog is a simple reporting tool that enables both customers and project teams to monitor the progress of work against the agreed features in each iteration. Although requirements backlogs can vary in format and complexity – depending on the nature of the work that the team is doing – the basic components of a requirements backlog are:

*   A top-down priority list of the features that the team is scheduled to work on
*   Grouping of these features into iterations that indicate when the work for each is scheduled to be completed
*   Tracking the progress of each feature by recording:
    o   When the work is actually undertaken
    o   The amount of work remaining to complete (i.e. fulfill) the requirement.
*   Graphical tools that visually depict the amount of overall work remaining for the project team and the estimated time in which the work will be completed (i.e. burndown charts).

Figure 2 shows an example of a simple requirements backlog[40]

---

[40] Adapted from the Simple Product Backlog example courtesy of *www.AgileSoftwareDevelopment.com.*

Product website requirements backlog

ID	Value (x$100)	Description	1	2	3	4	5	6
		Effort needed for minimum requirements	107	48	28	0	0	0
1	50	Reserve domain name	5	0	0	0	0	0
2	50	Design website look and feel	12	0	0	0	0	0
3	20	Create product information pages	2	0	0	0	0	0
4	30	Design site structure	12	0	0	0	0	0
5	20	Design navigation menu options	4	0	0	0	0	0
Iteration 1		*Goal: Set up basic product website*						
6	80	Create online product order form	16	6	2	0	0	0
16	10	Add downloadable PDF order form	2	1	0	0	0	0
17	10	Create help pages for order form	-	2	0	0	0	0
7	50	Submit orders to internal system	16	3	1	0	0	0
8	20	Notify users if system is down	2	2	0	0	0	0
9	50	Create order confirmation page	4	3	3	0	0	0
Iteration 2		*Goal: Process product orders on website*						
10	80	Process payments with order form	16	15	6	0	0	0
11	40	Allow customers to calculate prices before ordering	8	8	8	0	0	0
12	20	Advise customer on payment status	4	4	4	0	0	0
13	50	Provide receipt for payment	4	4	4	0	0	0
Iteration 3		*Goal: Process payments with product orders*						
		Milestone: Minimum requirements for product orders with payment	8	8	8	8	8	8
14	5	Allow customers to customize product	4	4	4	4	4	4
15	3	Provide interactive product selection guide	4	4	4	4	4	4
18	2	Display links to related products	4	4	4	4	4	4
Iteration 4		*Goal: Add services to help customer select products*						
		Milestone: Product orders with additional customer services						
		Effort in the whole backlog	123	64	44	16	16	16

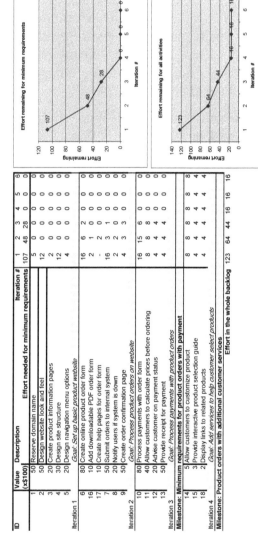

http://agilesoftwaredevelopment.com/scrum/simple-product-backlog

Figure 2: Agile tools: Simple requirements backlog

The content of the requirements backlog is managed and updated by all members of the project team and the customer:

- Customers are responsible for maintaining the list of requirements in top-down priority order.
- The customers and the project team collectively determine the iteration in which each requirement will be delivered as part of the iteration planning session.
- Progress tracking on the work for each requirement is maintained by the project team through the day-to-day recording of their work in the delivery backlog. (Where the details in the delivery backlog are rolled up to provide the overall calculations used in the requirements backlog.)

The requirements backlog becomes a shared tool for the customer, all members of the project team, and management to keep track of the overall status of their work. It combines textual detail (on the left) and visual indicators (on the right) to give the department a snapshot of the team's progress at any point in time, without requiring the team to develop separate corporate status reports.

Tracking day-to-day work in the delivery backlog

The delivery backlog is a dynamic reporting tool that enables project teams to monitor and manage their actual day-to-day work in far more detail than the requirements backlog allows. Where the requirements backlog is a tool for customers to record, prioritize and track the progress of business requirements overall, the delivery backlog is a tool for project team members to record and track their *actual work* and *progress* against the detailed tasks for each iteration.

At the end of each iteration planning session, the customers and the project team agree on the subset of high-priority features that will be actioned in the upcoming iteration (i.e. "draw the line" in the top-down priority order of tasks).

These agreed features are transferred from the requirements backlog to a list of corresponding tasks in the delivery backlog for the project team members to action.

For example, if one of the features in the requirements backlog for building a website is to "provide two levels of menu options for easier user navigation", the corresponding task entries in the delivery backlog may be:

- Research menu scripting options
- Check browser compatibility
- Build dynamic second-level menus.

In effect, the *features* that are listed in the requirements backlog become *actionable work* in the delivery backlog. These are the specific tasks that the project team will need to do in order to deliver each agreed business requirement for that iteration.

Figure 3 shows an example of a simple delivery backlog[41].

---

[41] Adapted from the Simple Sprint Backlog example courtesy of www.AgileSoftwareDevelopment.com.

Product website delivery backlog

Iteration 3 Goal: Process payments with product orders

ID	Task		Day in iteration / Effort remaining												
		1	2	3	4	5	6	7	8	9	10	11	12	13	14
		32	32	31	28	26	22	22	21	18	16	16	16	16	16
10	**Process payments with order form**														
	Build interface to credit card processing system	8	8	7	6	6	5	5	5	4	4	3	3	3	3
	Build security layer	4	4	3	3	3	3	3	3	3	3	3	3	3	3
	Queue payments	1	1	1	1	1	1	1	1	1	1	1	1	1	1
	Store payment history	3	3	3	2	2	2	2	2	1	1	1	1	1	1
11	**Allow customers to calculate prices before ordering**														
	Create pricing database	2	2	4	4	4	4	4	4	4	4	4	4	4	4
	Build price calculation form	2	2	2	2	1	1	1	1	1	0	0	0	0	0
	Display pricing options	1	1	0	0	0	0	1	1	0	1	1	1	1	1
	Validate form	3	3	3	3	2	2	2	2	1	1	1	1	1	1
12	**Advise customer on payment status**														
	Retrieve status from credit card processing system	3	3	3	2	2	2	2	1	1	2	2	2	1	1
	Present status to customer	1	1	2	2	2	2	1	1	1	1	2	2	1	2
13	**Provide receipt for payment**														
	Build receipt display screen	1	1	0	0	0	0	0	0	0	0	0	0	0	0
	Retrieve payment identification number	3	3	3	3	3	3	0	0	0	0	0	0	0	0

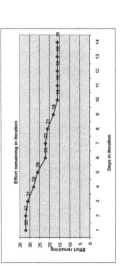

http://agilesoftwaredevelopment.com/scrum/simple-sprint-backlog

Figure 3: Agile tools: Simple delivery backlog

The delivery backlog shown in the diagram represents the progress of the project team at day nine of iteration three. Effort remaining is tracked in a similar way to how the requirements backlog is tracked, with:

- Reducing left-to-right values for each task generally indicating that progress has been made
- Unchanging left-to-right values for each task generally indicating that there has been no progress
- Increasing left-to-right values for each task generally indicating that the task is more complex or time-consuming than originally estimated.

The critical thing to notice in the delivery backlog is the ID number assigned to each task in the leftmost column. These numbers corresponds to the equivalent "Activity ID" in the requirements backlog, allowing the "effort remaining" details in the delivery backlog to be *automatically* carried over into the requirements backlog for real-time status reporting. This means that all that the project team needs to do during the course of each iteration is to maintain the daily "effort remaining" values for the individual tasks within each of the activities scheduled.

The content of the delivery backlog is managed and updated by all members of the project team on a daily basis. Maintaining the progress information in the delivery backlog is not an added overhead for the project team members; it is an essential part of their own self-management. The fact that management and customers can also use the delivery backlog tool (and the corresponding requirements backlog) to track the team's progress is an added benefit from the project team's perspective. It means that they will have little (or no) additional paperwork to complete at the end of each month.

The power of the "burndown" chart

The requirements backlog and delivery backlog examples shown in the previous sections both include graphical charts, known as burndown charts, that indicate the project team's progress (and effort remaining) for each iteration. This enables the project team to track the *velocity* (i.e. the productivity rates) of their work.

In the requirements backlog, the burndown chart on the top right-hand side provides a visual representation of the amount of work (effort) that is remaining for the project team to achieve the minimum requirements; the burndown chart on the bottom right-hand side provides a visual representation of the amount of work (effort) that is remaining for the project team to achieve *all* of the listed requirements for the initiative.

In the delivery backlog, the burndown chart at the bottom left-hand side provides a visual representation of the amount of work (effort) that is remaining for the project team to achieve all of the tasks *within that iteration*.

Combined, these burndown charts enable the customers and the project team to track velocity within and across iterations. This provides the team with two valuable tools:

- A self-management tool that allows project teams to track their delivery pace during each iteration
- An estimation tool that can assist project teams in determining the amount of work that they can reasonably expect to deliver in future iterations (based on the "yesterday's weather" productivity rates for previous

work done by the project team that was of an equivalent size and complexity).

The use of velocity information provides a tool for project teams to confidently make estimations based on real accounts of their historical productivity levels (not "guesstimates"). It assures the project team that the work that they have committed to is achievable – and it generally results in far more realistic productivity levels in the actual work completed for each iteration.

The power of velocity tracking, however, is not limited to estimations of future work. It is an equally valuable tool for project teams to track and manage their work during each iteration against the levels of productivity that they committed to at the start of the iteration.

Tracking velocity in current iterations allows the project team to keep tabs on its own status by comparing the level of outputs that they had expected to deliver (doing similar work) against the level of outputs that they are currently generating. If the project team is producing fewer outputs than expected, this may be a red flag for the team members to step back and see what might be causing the slowdown. For example, in the current iteration, customers may not be as responsive to project team member questions as they had been in the past due to end-of-year financial reporting commitments. Equally, if the team determines that they are moving at a *faster* pace than expected, they may be able to confidently commit to a greater number of tasks at the next iteration planning session – or even begin work on a few features that were directly "below the line" in the requirements backlog.

The content of burndown charts can be automatically updated based on the progress information that the project team records in the delivery backlog each day. This enables the project team to review and track their velocity *without requiring additional work* to collect this information.

The real-time executive dashboard

In addition to progress reporting through requirements backlogs, delivery backlogs and burndown charts, Agile approaches provide management with executive dashboard reports that summarize the work within (and across) Agile teams for easy progress monitoring across the organization. Executive dashboards are similar in design to standard dashboards in corporate reporting tools. Corporate reporting dashboards provide management with an "at-a-glance" visual summary of key activities in the organization (usually actual progress against financial KPIs). Agile executive dashboards also provide "at-a-glance" visual summary information, but the focus is on measuring *real productivity gains* by summarizing the work completed and the work remaining for each Agile team across their iterations.

Figure 4 shows an example of an executive dashboard tool that management can use to monitor the progress of Agile work.

Product website executive dashboard

At-a-glance core requirements

Core requirement	% Complete	Value earned	Value remaining	Estimated completion
Online product orders	80	$9,600	$2,400	Iteration 3
Order confirmation	93	$10,300	$700	Iteration 3
Internal order processing	94	$4,700	$300	Iteration 3
Payment processing	67	$6,700	$3,300	Iteration 3
Status tracking	0	$0	$4,000	Iteration 3

Requirements burndown charts

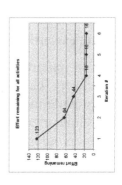

Expected versus earned business value

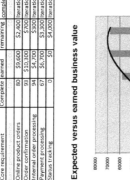

Figure 4: Agile tools: Executive dashboard

In this executive dashboard tool, summary information is broken down into three mandatory sections:

1. **At-a-glance core requirements:** show the progress of Agile work against each key executive-level objective for the Agile team
2. **Requirements burndown charts:** show the overall progress of the Agile team based on the amount of work that they have completed and the amount of work that is remaining against each milestone
3. **Expected versus earned business value:** shows the overall progress of the Agile team based on the business value of the work that they have completed and the business value of the work that is remaining.

There are other optional sections that Agile teams may choose to include in the executive dashboard if they are relevant to the work that the team is doing, such as:

- A "work breakdown structure" (WBS) that visually depicts the correlation and dependencies between each key executive-level objective for the project
- A "key information" text area for other important status and context information that management needs to be aware of, including:
  o Key achievements
  o Key decisions
  o Known issues
  o Critical risks.

Project teams can adapt the executive dashboard for each initiative to suit the specific requirements of their work, the standards for the organization overall, or the preferences of individual managers.

As with the velocity tracking tools, most of the information in the executive dashboard tool is *automatically generated* based on the progress information that the project team records in the delivery backlog each day. However, some of the optional sections (such as the WBS and the "key information" area), where included, can require manual maintenance by the project team.

The WBS, which can be handcrafted by the team at the start of the work, only requires updating when the status (or nature) of the key objectives changes – which is generally apparent at the end of each iteration planning session. The "key information" area, however, may require more frequent maintenance based on the critical information that arises during the course of each iteration. In some cases, project teams have opted to link this section of the executive dashboard to a dynamic issues log that is maintained in a centralized area, which the team updates every time key information arises (rather than waiting until the end of each iteration to update these details). This enables management to get a realistic snapshot of Agile work at any point in time, not just as part of their monthly reports. (How many corporate reports are you aware of that can give you real-time updates on the amount of business value that employees are – and are not – generating in their ongoing work?)

It is important to note that the example provided shows the work that is being tracked for one Agile project; however, executive dashboards can provide tracking information at any level of detail, including a visual summary of the work being done across *all* Agile projects.

Early and continuous delivery tracking

One way in which Agile approaches differ significantly from traditional business practices is in their ability to deliver business value to the organization *from the first iteration.* Because the work that the project team delivers is *functional outputs* (not thought papers or prototypes), the work that is delivered at the end of each iteration is often available for the organization to use immediately. This means that the organization can expect to receive early and ongoing benefits from the department's Agile work.

Similarly, the nature of Agile tracking and reporting tools means that the department receives *early and continuous status information* regarding Agile work. Management does not have to wait for a monthly report to know that there is substantial progress in (or key issues with) the work that the teams are doing. Equally, the customers and project team members do not have to wait until the end of the month to see status information that can indicate significant problems in the work that they are doing. Instead of status reporting being a one-off historical view of work each month (or even each quarter), Agile tracking and reporting tools provide the team members (and the organization) with *real-time feedback* on their progress – and *real-time flags* when action is required.

CHAPTER 11: MEASURING AGILE SUCCESS

Monitoring progress

Agile approaches work on the basis that the best way for the department to monitor the progress of work is *not* to receive endless status reports from the project team, but to review the fully functional, fully tested capabilities delivered by the team in each iteration (i.e. the *tangible outputs* of the team's work) as the primary measure of progress. This is because status reports are often time-consuming, generally sanitized for management review and can be designed to give the reader of the report a false sense of security that things are progressing on track. Tangible outputs, on the other hand, are *irrefutable indicators* of the ongoing success or failure of each project team's activities.

This means that, when Agile work is done in four-week iterations, the department has at least one time each month when key stakeholders (management and the customer) can get a *hands-on review* of the team's outputs – and track the completed work against the originally-agreed objectives. Where more stringent monitoring of the team's progress is required, Agile work can be reduced to two-week iterations. This allows stakeholders to get a hands-on review of completed work every other week – and to request rework if the outputs do not meet their expectations[42].

In addition to tracking the progress at the end of each iteration, teams use Agile management tools, such as

---

[42] With the caveat that stakeholders need to scale their expectations to work that the team can reasonably complete in a two-week period, and not expect that four weeks' worth of work will be completed in a two-week timeframe.

delivery backlogs and burndown charts, to provide the organization with status information regarding their work *throughout* each iteration. (*See Chapter 10: Using Agile Tools for further detail on the use of these tools.*)

These tools can be made available to anyone in the organization with an interest in the project team's work – which means that customers, operational managers and executives are all able to get daily updates on the work that the project team has accomplished, along with an understanding of what work is remaining.

Measuring value

Equally important to monitoring the progress of ongoing Agile work is quantifying and measuring the *business value* of the work produced by each project team. Measuring the value of project work is a critical factor in confirming whether teams are delivering the highest-priority, highest-value capabilities in each solution. It is not about the *quantity* of features released in each iteration – or even the *amount of hours* that the team spent working on the project in that iteration; it is about the *business value* generated by the features that they deliver.

In the *Measuring productivity by outputs* section of *Chapter 10: Using Agile Tools*, it was identified that executive dashboards and backlogs can be used to track both the business value that has been generated by the team in each iteration as well as the pending business value of their remaining work. Having this information allows management to both quantify the value that has been generated by the department within and across all of their Agile projects and to determine the best use of available resources for ongoing work (based on the relative value of the remaining work in each initiative). This business-value information can also be used, when needed, to acquire ongoing executive support for Agile approaches, which provides departments with a level of management reporting – and justification for ongoing funding – that is rarely available in traditional software development methods.

There is, however, another important distinction between Agile approaches and traditional software development methods. In a traditional business environment, stopping an initiative after two months generally means that the work undertaken up to that point is filed away until a future time when the work is resurrected (if ever). In many cases, this half-completed work sits indefinitely on a network drive until it is moved into an archive. Worse still, by the time the initiative is resurrected, the amount of time that has passed may make the work obsolete.

In an Agile environment, stopping an initiative after two months means that the organization is in a position to get eight weeks' worth of valuable deliverables. This means that the customer can get a portion of the required functionality, even if the initiative is never resumed. It may not be the full functionality that was originally envisioned, but a partially functioning solution is far better than a pile of screen mock-ups (or a scoping paper that analyzes how the work might be done, along with a detailed project plan). This means that the organization is regularly in a position to realize the return on their investment sooner than traditional software development activities would normally deliver (e.g. business-value outputs every month versus every six months). Moreover, because that portion represents the *highest-priority work* for the organization, there are times when receiving only these initial outcomes is sufficient for the organization to have achieved its intended objectives.

Signs that the team is off-track

The real-time tracking of work progress in Agile approaches provides the organization with another significant advantage over traditional software development methods: immediate risk identification and mitigation.

Key issues that can affect the project team's productivity levels are immediately apparent in the tools that track the velocity of the team's work. If the project team is producing outputs in an iteration at a significantly slower velocity than they did in a previous iteration with equivalent work, this could be a strong indication that the team is encountering issues that are limiting their productivity. Although Agile tracking and reporting tools cannot determine whether the source of the issue is a lack of skilled resources, insufficient participation from key stakeholders, inadequate tools or other organizational factors, a reduction in velocity *can* prompt the customer, the team members or their management to take action to investigate the source of the problem. Furthermore, the real-time nature of these tools means that the investigation and mitigation does not need to wait until the end of the calendar month – or the quarter – before being actioned.

It should also be noted that velocity measurements are deliberately based upon the activities that can be achieved in *normal working hours*. If the work scheduled for an iteration requires overtime in order to be completed by the end of the iteration, the Agile team needs to either:

- Scope down the scheduled work for that iteration (i.e. raise the line in the requirements backlog), so that work can be completed in normal working hours, or
- Break down larger tasks into smaller ones that can be achieved in the iteration without requiring overtime.

The equivalent guideline is true as work is progressing throughout the iteration. If the project team's velocity is slower than expected for that iteration – and it is not due to an external issue – the team will need to *scope down* the work that they are doing by postponing lower-priority activities until there is sufficient time. (Or by supplementing the team with additional resources where possible.) Aiming to deliver the pre-determined list of outcomes through evening and weekend work should only be considered an option in extremely rare circumstances.

Controlling budget expenditure

Anyone who has ever managed a traditional software project knows firsthand that there is no direct correlation between budget expenditure and progress. Managing a project budget is necessary to meet departmental and contractual obligations – and to ensure the availability of adequate funds for ongoing work – but it is not, in and of itself, a measure of success.

Chapter 14: Budgeting for Agile Work provides you with guidelines for managing Agile work within established budgets, as well as calculating future budget expenditures. This section focuses instead on how you can use Agile approaches to successfully *control* that budget expenditure.

One of the most insidious aspects of traditional software development methods is that the true progress – and value – of project work is generally not known until the full solution is released into the acceptance-testing environment. Prior to acceptance testing, you can monitor the hours spent on the project – even the lines of code generated by the project team – but there is no way to know whether the budget expended to date truly represents the equivalent percentage of production-ready work. In other words, there is no way to know whether having spent 75% of your available budget means that 75% of the required work has been successfully completed.

With Agile work, the team provides fully functional, fully tested, production-ready capabilities in each iteration, which means that the customer has the opportunity at the end of each iteration to advise whether the delivered work meets their requirements. Not only does this give you the confidence of knowing whether the budget expended for that iteration correlates with a corresponding percentage of the solution – it gives the customer the opportunity to stop (or adjust) work that is not on track well before ongoing budget dollars are spent. All of this means that the amount of system capability that needs to be reworked – and the associated budget expenditure – is contained.

Receiving production-ready capabilities at the end of each iteration also provides the opportunity for the customer to identify when all of the core requirements for the initiative have been delivered, which may be well before the full budget allocated for this work has been expended.

Knowing that the team has met the core requirements for the initiative gives stakeholders the option to either let team members continue delivering capabilities for the original initiative, or reallocate funds and resources to other high-priority work in the department. This means that the completion of project work can be based on the team delivering every outcome that stakeholders consider essential, instead of maintaining project teams to meet pre-determined timeframes or budget allocations.

There is another area where Agile work helps you to ensure the most effective use of your available budget – minimizing the time that the team spends on low business-value activities.

Generating business value has as much to do with what the team delivers as what it *does not deliver* in the process. Any time that the team works on low business-value activities (including extensive status reporting) is time that could have been better spent delivering *actual value* to the organization. Miscommunication, extensive delays in obtaining management approvals and a lack of quality control processes can create an atmosphere of misaligned deliverables and rework – which results in wasted resource time and costs for the department. Equally wasteful is having the team do *more* work than is required to satisfy an objective (commonly known in the Agile world as *over-production* or *over-delivery*).

The very nature of Agile approaches means that teams do not have the time (or luxury) to focus on hypothetical situations. The short iterations and "Apply, Inspect, Adapt" mindset of Agile approaches mean that project teams are not in a position to go too far down the wrong path before the customer (or others) get them back on track. It also means that project teams are not in a position to over-deliver in preparation for what the customer *might* require;

they have just enough time available to deliver what they know the customer really needs.

Continuous improvement

A key component of Agile approaches is the relentless effort to regularly review – and improve – the work undertaken by the team. Towards this, Agile approaches incorporate *retrospectives* as a standard activity in each iteration.

Retrospectives are dedicated times when the project team can step back and review the work that was undertaken in the previous iteration. Retrospectives provide the stakeholders and the project team with a chance to collectively reflect on both the good and bad aspects of the work that they did. The intent of the exercise is to recognize those processes (and people) that were particularly effective in the previous iteration; and to identify challenges and problems that need to be addressed, in order to improve the work in subsequent iterations.

It should be noted that retrospectives are *not* intended to be blaming sessions or endless discussions on why something did not go as expected. This is why retrospectives should not be day-long activities. (In most cases, they take about an hour.) Keeping the retrospective timing to an hour avoids the potential for them becoming extended "think tanks", where teams spend endless amounts of time contemplating the meaning of life. Retrospectives are brainstorming sessions where issues (and resolutions) get identified, prioritized, assigned ownership and actioned.

One last comment about the structure of retrospectives: although managers are welcome to attend these sessions, they need to respect the fact that retrospectives are *team-driven* exercises. The intent of the retrospective is for the customer and the team members – who have been actively involved in the process – to be able to freely discuss (and resolve) their issues. This is why, if managers choose to attend retrospectives, they need to be prepared to go there as observers only.[43]

---

[43] There is an argument to say that the mere presence of managers or executives in a retrospective (even as observers) may unintentionally affect the dynamic of the exercise by making attendees feel more self-conscious about discussing their concerns – or less likely to want to expose what may be perceived by management as weaknesses in the process. Therefore, managers need to make a judgment call on whether it would be more valuable for them to attend a retrospective, or to be briefed on the outcomes of the exercise after the event.

CHAPTER 12: ALIGNING AGILE WITH YOUR CORPORATE CULTURE

The most important factor in successful Agile adoption (and expansion) is aligning it to the culture, structures and constraints of your organization. Even the most effective Agile project work risks losing executive support if it cannot meet the overarching management, compliance and administrative structures established by the organization, which include:

- Project management frameworks (such as the PMBOK®, PRINCE2® and ITIL®)
- Corporate reporting
- Budget management
- Contract management
- Staffing procedures
- Performance metrics.

So, unless you are in the unique position of being able to adjust your organizational structures to suit the flexibility of Agile approaches[44], you will need to find a way for your team's Agile work to comply with these corporate standards. Thankfully, this is an achievable goal, although it may take some creative thinking to make it work within your specific organizational constraints.

The following chapters address the specific challenges of aligning Agile approaches within the project frameworks, budgeting structures, reporting requirements, staffing

---

[44] As was achieved at BT Innovate and Design.

guidelines and other constraints of your organization. These chapters are intended to provide you with realistic and achievable approaches for achieving this alignment by advising on both:

*   The *ideal model*, where Agile approaches are readily accepted and corporate structures are adapted to support these approaches, and
*   The *reality model*, where you need to work within existing organizational structures with minimal opportunity for accommodating the flexibility of Agile approaches.

Importantly, each of these chapters offers *a range of options* to address the constraints, enabling you to find the most suitable approaches for your department (i.e. those that will be the least time-consuming for you and your staff and that have the greatest overlap with current work); and giving you the flexibility to adapt selected approaches as the organization becomes more familiar with (and more supportive of) Agile approaches.

CHAPTER 13: MANAGING AGILE WITHIN YOUR EXISTING PROJECT FRAMEWORKS

Overview

The word "project" is a fantastically broad term that covers everything from event planning, to delivering small and large software solutions, to the construction of a new building. It is the abstract nature of this word that forces:

* Project management frameworks, such as the PMBOK® and PRINCE2®
* Process management frameworks, such as CMMI® and ITIL®, and
* Quality management frameworks

to be high-level enough to be equally applicable to projects of all sizes across multiple industries and organizational activities. This means that these frameworks primarily focus on constraining work to meet identified *management objectives* (such as time, budget and risk management), but they do not (and arguably *cannot*) significantly focus on *how* this work is undertaken. It is this lack of specificity of the work itself that allows Agile approaches to readily fit within these structures.

One of the keys to successfully delivering Agile work within existing project frameworks is differentiating between the *strategic objectives* of the project and the *operational activities* within it. If a software project is defined to deliver *strategic business outcomes* (such as cost reductions, increases in productivity, or revenue generation), then the detail of exactly *how* these outcomes will be achieved can be left to the discretion of the project team and the customer. However, if the same software project is defined with hundreds of pages of detailed operational specifications, then the project team is generally handcuffed to the outcome from the beginning, with little room to adjust the work as it evolves (and, consequently, a limited ability for the team to use Agile approaches in the work).

Therefore, one of the critical factors in complying with existing frameworks is defining the deliverables to be based on *strategic business objectives* – not on detailed functionality. For example, the executive office might establish the following constraints for a planned IT project:

- It must be delivered within the $120,000 allocated budget
- It must be delivered and in production use by the end of the third quarter
- It must achieve the following business objectives:
  - To decrease order form completion time by 25%
  - To decrease order processing time by 20%
  - To keep customers aware of the status of their orders – from initial form submission to order fulfillment
  - To encourage customers to submit future orders.

Nothing about these constraints stops your department from strategically working directly with the business areas (i.e. the customer) to define the details of how the objectives will be achieved, or from achieving the objectives by delivering multiple smaller releases of functional software throughout the specified timeframe.

13: Managing Agile within Your Existing Project Frameworks

The following sections identify how strategies such as these can be used to align Agile work with a range of common project, process and quality management frameworks.

PMBOK®

The Project Management Body of Knowledge (PMBOK®), issued by the Project Management Institute (PMI), is one of the most commonly used approaches for implementing best practices in project management. It focuses on managing nine core knowledge areas[45]:

1. Integration
2. Scope
3. Time
4. Cost
5. Quality
6. Human resources
7. Communication
8. Risk
9. Procurement

across five key process groups:

1. *Initiating* the project
2. *Planning* the project
3. *Executing* the project
4. *Monitoring* and *Controlling* the project
5. *Closing* the project.

At first glance, the structure of the PMBOK® appears to closely align with traditional project management

---

[45] *A Guide to the Project Management Body of Knowledge (PMBOK® Guide)*, PMI (2010).

approaches, focusing heavily on upfront planning as a way to control outcomes and minimize risk. This initial appearance is supported by the fact that ongoing project management in the PMBOK® is based on measuring the progress of the project against the *originally defined* objectives. Towards this, the project management organization (PMO) serves as the overarching governance body, which oversees project work and monitors the delivery of project outcomes on behalf of the organization. Key project measurements are based on elapsed time, budget expenditure, resource utilization, risk management, and the delivery of outputs against agreed milestones. A "successful" project is one that delivers the agreed outputs within the timeframe and budget as originally identified in the project charter.

Therefore, upon initial review, it would appear as though the structure of the PMBOK® contravenes several of the core Agile principles identified in *Chapter 1: What is Agile?* – most notably the principle to *replace upfront planning with incremental planning*. That is, until you look more closely at exactly what the PMBOK® requires, and how it can be adapted to fit the needs of each project – and each organization.

At its core, the PMBOK® provides a *framework* for delivering outcomes to achieve an overarching corporate or management objective for the organization – such as developing a product, delivering a program, or implementing a services initiative. The PMBOK® is designed to be applicable to a broad range of projects (e.g. building construction, software development or government initiatives) across a number of industry sectors. Accordingly, it cannot (and, therefore, does not) endeavor to prescribe *how* specific activities are undertaken by the project team, as long as the outputs of that team:

- Adhere to the agreed budget and time constraints of the project
- Achieve the agreed business objectives.

This is exactly where the PMBOK®'s methodologies and Agile approaches truly complement each other.

A second glance at the PMBOK® reveals a number of nuances that are less evident to traditional PMBOK® practitioners, but provide a valid pathway for converging the PMBOK® and Agile approaches in the successful delivery of software projects.

Flexibility in PMBOK® Planning

The *Planning* process group includes two fundamental principles that allow project work to be structured around Agile approaches:

1. **Progressive elaboration:** Within the Planning process group, the PMBOK® identifies *progressive elaboration* as the need for projects to adjust and evolve their original plans to incorporate emerging information as the project progresses. Progressive elaboration provides the foundation (and justification) for using Agile approaches in the PMBOK® project work (as, by their very nature, Agile approaches are designed around supporting the *evolution of work* throughout the project timeline).

2. **Rolling wave planning:** Within the Planning process group, the PMBOK® further identifies *rolling wave planning* as executing project work in short iterations,

with plans adjusted to reflect information that emerges as the project progresses. This aligns directly with *incremental planning* in Agile work (with the notable exception that incremental planning does not work to an agreed upfront specification).

This acknowledgement of (and allowance for) flexibility in project planning means that organizations *can* identify their PMBOK® work in the context of agreed Agile approaches (such as Scrum or FDD™), with outcomes defined as iterative deliverables of the highest-priority software capabilities, as agreed with the business.

Flexibility in PMBOK® Execution

The fact that the PMBOK® is not prescriptive about *how* project work is undertaken (as long as that work achieves the agreed objectives) provides an equally powerful opportunity for introducing Agile within this framework. The ideal structure includes:

- A project plan that is designed around iterative releases
- Inputs defined as prioritized business requirements for each iteration
- Outputs defined as iterative releases of functional software that includes the highest-priority software capabilities agreed with the business.

In this ideal model, the project team has the flexibility to use their preferred Agile approaches with the full awareness and support of the PMO; however, there are ways in which the team can implement Agile practices without this explicit support (*see the No support option below for further detail*).

Where there is explicit support for the use of Agile approaches, the PMO has a range of options in providing oversight of project work: they can choose to act as the hands-on business representative (e.g. the customer), who prioritizes requirements and reviews the output of each iteration in detail; or, if they are more time-constrained, they can monitor the progress of project work through Agile reporting tools (e.g. executive dashboards), attending iterative review sessions where possible and/or receiving formal updates from the project team.

So, how do you align the PMBOK® and Agile approaches within the specific requirements and constraints of your organization? There are three ways to achieve this, depending on how willing your PMO is to allow Agile approaches to be used to deliver project work:

Full support

Where you are fortunate enough to have the full support of the PMO in using Agile approaches, the easiest way to align Agile work with the PMBOK® is to start off by defining the project charter at a strategic level – not an operational one. Key to this is defining project objectives as measurable *business goals*, such as increased online sales, fewer customer complaints, or reduced overhead costs in fulfilling customer orders. The mechanisms by which these goals are achieved are then left to the discretion of strategically selected key business representatives, who prioritize and manage ongoing project work against the software capabilities that they believe will best achieve these outcomes. It should be noted that the project charter could, where needed, specify the involvement of selected key business representatives as a mandate from the project authority.

Once the project charter has been established, the planning process uses the principles of *progressive elaboration* and *rolling wave planning* to define project work as a series of iterations within an overall agreed timeframe and budget. The scope of capabilities that is delivered within these constraints is then left to the discretion of the customer. (Further guidance on managing Agile projects within established time and budget constraints is provided in *Chapters 14 to 16.*)

The PMBOK® planning activities can also be aligned with common Agile practices, such as the dedicating of the first iteration of a Scrum project ("iteration zero") to investigating the business requirements, proposed technologies and other background research necessary, in order to decompose the requirements in a work breakdown structure (WBS), identify the critical path, provide estimates for proposed work, and identify risks.

Project Execution is then undertaken by the project team using the selected Agile approaches as described above, with Monitoring and Controlling achieved through real-time management reporting on progress and iterative reviews of functional software throughout the duration of the project.

Project Closing is undertaken in conjunction with the final agreed iterative deliverables for the project (or earlier, where business objectives have already been achieved by delivered software). Standard PMBOK® project-closing activities can be undertaken at this point, along with Agile retrospective reviews undertaken by the project team, so that they can gain greater insight into what did (and did not) work well in the project delivery.

Trial support

Where the PMO is hesitant to provide full support for the use of Agile approaches across the project, it may be possible for you to negotiate for a compromise position, such as trialing Agile approaches for a fixed period of time (e.g. the first three months of the project) to see if they are happy with the outcomes. Critical to this is getting agreement from the PMO to have the most current prioritized list of system capabilities drive the project team's work during this trial period, instead of a detailed upfront specification.

At the end of the trial period, if the PMO is happy with the capabilities delivered through the Agile work, they then have the option of allowing Agile approaches to continue to be used for the remainder of the project (or of extending the trial period).

However, despite the delivery of high-priority functional software, the PMO may still be unsure about committing ongoing resources without a signed-off document of detailed system capabilities. If this is the case (and there is no opportunity to extend the trial period), you may have to resort to detailing the remaining software functionality as a signed-off specification, and referring to the *No support* option below.

It is interesting to note the correlation between how much the PMO *trusts* the project team, and how willing they are to allow (and to continue to allow) project work to be done using Agile approaches. The more that the PMO insists upon having a detailed upfront specification, the more likely it is that they feel the need to control the outcomes because they do not trust the project team to deliver. If this is the case, there may be an opportunity for you, as a director, to negotiate for added review sessions and greater visibility of the team's work, instead of foregoing the opportunity for the project team to use Agile approaches altogether.

No support

If the circumstances of your organization (or the hesitancy of the PMO) mean that neither of the above two approaches are achievable, you may need to resort to "Agile by stealth", where the team effectively uses Agile practices as much as possible to produce agreed outcomes, and then retrofits these outcomes into deliverables that align with the agreed outputs for project work. For example, it may still be possible for the project team to collaborate with users in software design, hold daily stand-up meetings to increase team communication, and undertake Test-Driven Development to increase the quality of the delivered software. There may even be the opportunity for the project team to continue to deliver fully functional capabilities on an iterative basis, and then "package" the outputs into releases that correspond with the agreed specifications (even where the project charter and planning work do not allow for adjustments to the functionality to align with emerging information).

Using "Agile by stealth" is the least beneficial way for the project team to comply with the PMBOK®, as it:

- Minimizes the ability of the developed software to produce continually relevant high business-value returns
- Limits the flexibility of the organization to respond to emergent organizational, industry or technology information
- Creates significant overheads (and delays) in approving and implementing software changes
- Requires project teams to produce outputs that add little to no business value (e.g. status reports that effectively repeat the progress information that is already being tracked in backlogs, executive dashboards, etc.)

Therefore, it is strongly preferred that you, as a director, take the initiative to present the benefits of Agile approaches to the PMO (*see Chapter 3: The Core Business Benefits of Agile*), and negotiate trialing Agile for a contained timeframe within the project work as described in the *Trial support* section above.

Further information on the use of Agile and PMBOK® is provided in Mike Griffiths' paper: *Using Agile Alongside the PMBOK®*, PMI Global Congress 2004[46], and in the resources listed in *Chapter 21: More Information on Agile.*

PRINCE2®

The PRojects IN Controlled Environments 2 (PRINCE2®) method provides a framework that allows organizations to more effectively manage the costs, timeframe, scope, quality and risks of each project, in accordance with its own

---

[46] *Using Agile Alongside the PMBOK®*, Griffiths M (2004):
http://leadinganswers.typepad.com/files/using-agile-alongside-the-PMBOK_paper.pdf.

overarching principles, themes and processes. Like the PMBOK®, the PRINCE2® method is structured at a reasonably high level, allowing the details of each project to fit within the overall framework, as described on the PRINCE2® official website:

"PRINCE2® isolates the management aspects of project work from the specialist contributions, such as design, construction etc … providing a secure overall framework for project work."[47]

Originally, PRINCE2® included a significant number of controls to provide the project authority (e.g. the project board) with substantial influence over *how* project work was undertaken. More recently, however, PRINCE2® has undergone a review and refresh ("PRINCE2® 2009") in order to make the framework less prescriptive and more flexible, so that current project management approaches (such as Agile) can be better supported. This shift towards more modern project management approaches is evidenced in the following statement from the lead author of PRINCE2®:

"The emergence of Agile and iterative approaches to project management demonstrate there are challenges today that simply did not exist in 1996."[48]

---

[47] Adapted from *About PRINCE2®: The importance of projects*: www.prince-officialsite.com/AboutPRINCE2/AboutPRINCE2.aspx.
[48] *Managing and Directing Successful Projects with PRINCE2®* brochure: www.best-management-practice.com/gempdf/PRINCE2_2009_Overview_Brochure_June2011.pdf.

The problem is that, even with the release of PRINCE2® 2009, there is still a common misconception that Agile and PRINCE2® approaches contradict each other. It is true that the PRINCE2® 2009 framework is still somewhat more prescriptive than the PMBOK® framework – particularly in the encapsulation of project work into stages, with inputs, outputs and management controls defined at each stage of the work. However, at its heart, PRINCE2® 2009 is, like the PMBOK®, essentially a high-level framework that gives the project board the same discretion as the PMO in authorizing the use of Agile approaches for project implementation. This means that PRINCE2® 2009 and Agile methods effectively complement each other: PRINCE2® provides the overarching framework that ensures that project work continues to meet business objectives; Agile methods provide the mechanism for delivering relevant, high business-value outputs within this framework.

Therefore, much of the PMBOK® information provided in the previous section equally applies when aligning Agile with PRINCE2® 2009. The following notes specific areas of variation:

Flexibility in PRINCE2® 2009 Planning

Although PRINCE2® 2009 does not explicitly define *progressive elaboration* and *rolling wave planning* within the methodology, it does identify seven core principles that are intended to underpin all PRINCE2® 2009 project work[49]. These core principles include the following:

---

[49] *Project Management Based on PRINCE2®*, Hedeman B, Vis van Heemst G, Fredriksz H, Van Haren Publishing (2010).

- Tailor to suit the project environment
- Continued business justification
- Manage by stages
- Focus on products

all of which align to the key objectives of Agile approaches.

This gives the project board full discretion to authorize Agile approaches without contravening the core underlying principles of PRINCE2® 2009. It also allows them to approve the *project approach* in the project brief to be described at a reasonably high level. For example:

A project team will be assigned to develop the customer service portal in accordance with the requirements identified by the customer service manager and other key business areas. The success of the portal will be measured by monitoring its impact on the number of calls to customer service representatives, the duration of each call, and the level of satisfaction expressed in customer surveys.

instead of:

Eight developers will build the customer service portal using a service-oriented architecture on an Oracle® platform. The portal will provide a natural language search that allows customers to more easily find the information they need, an issue tracking system, and a live chat service.

If the willing participation of key business area representatives is a concern to the project team, the project brief can specify the involvement of specific people (or departments) as a pre-requisite for this work (and, ideally, as a mandate from the project board). The project brief can also allow for stages to be defined in accordance with iterative software delivery, as described in the following.

Flexibility in PRINCE2® 2009 Execution

The release of PRINCE2® 2009 offers an approach to project oversight that more readily allows project teams to adapt their work to meet the specific needs of each project (where this flexibility was not as evident in previous versions of PRINCE2®). Specifically, this means that PRINCE2® provides structure without prescribing (or prohibiting) the execution of project work in a way that best meets the need of the organization. This also means that the details of:

* What comprises each stage
* How success is defined and measured within each stage
* When a stage has achieved its expected results

are left to the discretion of the project team, under the direction and approval of the project board. This autonomy to determine *how* work is undertaken to achieve the agreed objectives is where Agile methodologies can fit in.

For software development projects, the flexibility of PRINCE2® 2009 enables:

* The project to be defined in a way that allows Agile methodologies to be used for the work at each stage, with corresponding work plans defined (and stage boundaries monitored) around Agile inputs (such as product backlogs), control mechanisms (such as

executive dashboards), and outputs (such as working software features)

• Stages to be structured around the iterative work that is being undertaken by the project team. However, as there are several management activities associated with the start and end of each stage, it is *not* recommended that organizations structure each Agile iteration as a separate stage. Instead, it is preferable to group the output from a number of iterations into a body of work that achieves a definitive (ideally measurable) business outcome. This is similar in intent to the way in which the production-ready capabilities across multiple Agile iterations can be grouped into one software release.

It should be noted that the same caveats on the use of Agile approaches in the PMBOK® methodology equally apply to the project board in PRINCE2® 2009. If you have the project board's full support, then the guidelines above will assist you in structuring your PRINCE2® project to support Agile work. However, if you have limited (or no) support from the project board, you will either need to negotiate for a trial period (e.g. one stage) or undertake work using "Agile by stealth", as described above.

For more information on PRINCE2®, see www.prince-officialsite.com/.

CMMI®

Capability Maturity Model Integration® (CMMI®) differs from the previous two frameworks in that it focuses on achieving the organization's business objectives by improving its *business processes* at a more holistic level –

moving work across the organization from uncontrolled to managed, reactive to proactive and unmeasured to quantitatively measured. Business processes in CMMI® progress through five maturity levels:

1. Initial
2. Managed
3. Defined
4. Quantitatively managed
5. Optimizing

with the ultimate goal of implementing optimal processes *across* the organization.

Like PMBOK® and PRINCE2®, however, CMMI® provides a *model* (i.e. a framework) to build upon – not detailed process definitions or standards. CMMI® is designed to provide organizations with a pathway towards continuous improvement in their processes *without* being prescriptive about the workings of each process, as evidenced in the following:

"Process areas are not processes themselves... [Processes] could be operating wherever and whenever and in whatever sequence necessary to perform the work of the business."[50]

CMMI®, therefore, provides sufficient flexibility for organizations to implement the *most suitable* processes to achieve their business objectives, which includes the use of Agile approaches in the delivery of IT software and services, where appropriate. This is similar in nature to the

---

[50] *CMMI® or Agile: Why Not Embrace Both!* Carnegie Mellon University and the Software Engineering Institute, founders of CMMI® (2008) www.sei.cmu.edu/library/abstracts/reports/08tn003.cfm.

previously described project frameworks, where overall governance is provided, but each area is given the discretion to choose the work method that could best achieve agreed objectives.

Agile and CMMI® have historically been perceived to be at opposite ends of the spectrum. For example, CMMI® is a top-down management directive, whereas the motivation for Agile tends to emerge from the grassroots level (i.e. the people doing the work on a day-to-day basis). Adding to this perceived disconnect is the fact that previous releases of CMMI® (and its predecessor, CMM®) were designed around mission-critical functionality in highly bureaucratic government environments, which led to CMM® having a strong emphasis on managing to *fixed upfront contract terms* and *significant levels of documentation*. This sharply contrasts with Agile approaches, which focus on *evolving business requirements* and building *just enough documentation* to communicate desired capabilities and to progress project work. Equally, both Agile and CMMI® have been subject to misunderstanding of terminology, lack of accurate information, and misuse, which has lead to the practitioners of each approach *misinterpreting* the other. Coupled with this has been an unjustified focus on the extremes of each (for example, either "CMMI® requires technical specifications to *always* be documented to a strict standard, e.g. MIL-STD-498", or "Agile requires *no* documentation at all").[51]

---

[51] Several of the ideas in the CMMI® section were inspired by *CMMI® or Agile: Why Not Embrace Both!* Carnegie Mellon University and the Software Engineering Institute, founders of CMMI® (2008) (*www.sei.cmu.edu/library/abstracts/reports/08tn003.cfm*), which provides excellent information on the topic.

In truth, however, both CMMI® and Agile are built upon the same core objective of achieving business goals using the most efficient methods possible. Agile does this by optimizing the work that is done within an individual project; CMMI® does this by implementing measures to optimize the work that is done for activities across the organization, including the work done in specific projects. Both approaches employ practices to focus organizations on continuous improvement (e.g. CMMI® lessons learned, Agile retrospectives). Adding to the synergy between these approaches is the fact that Agile work is more holistic than most traditional project methods, providing the project team with an *ongoing business context*, which demonstrates how the work that they are doing fits within the overall objectives of the organization. This context is provided through several Agile practices – most notably, the direct participation of the customer in the continuous identification, prioritization and confirmation of high-value capabilities. The result of this synergy is that not only *can* CMMI® and Agile work together, but there is an emerging community *actively* using both of these approaches in their work – this including industry discussion forums that are dedicated to the use of Agile approaches in a CMMI® organization[52].

It is important to note that CMMI® is more than just an overarching model that, when implemented correctly, allows Agile work to proceed without interference; CMMI® can *truly* complement the strengths of Agile by providing consistency within and across projects, and by making staff more amenable to (and better able to institutionalize) the

---

[52] Such as the *Agile and CMMI®* forum on LinkedIn (*www.linkedin.com*).

changes that result from Agile work.[53] This makes the concurrent use of both approaches a *higher-value proposition* for the organization than either approach provides on its own.

Flexibility in CMMI®

As identified above, the CMMI® model is *not* prescriptive about how specific processes are undertaken, as long as the overarching objective of moving organizations towards more optimal business processes is achieved. The flexibility of CMMI® allows organizations to implement CMMI® in a way that best suits the goals and dynamic of the organization environment; however, this same flexibility also gives organizations the ability to *over-specify* the work that is undertaken in support of CMMI®, particularly by mandating consistency at a very low level (e.g. detailed upfront documentation templates).

In order for organizations to effectively implement both CMMI® and Agile in the same environment, the CMMI® structures in that environment need to be flexible enough to allow for Agile methods to be utilized without being subject to excessive management structures that contravene its underlying principles. Ideally, Agile work can be explicitly defined as the process used for delivering IT software and services, with:

- **Measurements** tailored to the natural outputs of Agile work, including the progress metrics documented in

---

[53] *Scrum and CMMI® Level 5: A Magic Potion for Code Warriors,* Sutherland J, Jakobsen C, Johnson K, Agile Conference, Denver, CO (July 2005) http://jeffsutherland.com/2007/09/scrum-and-CMMI-level-5-magic-potion-for.html.

backlogs, burndown charts, work-in-progress charts and executive dashboards

*   **Feedback** based on the outcomes from iterative customer reviews of working capabilities
*   **Training** aligned to the organization's standard mechanisms for educating users in accordance with the release cycle across multiple Agile iterations
*   **Continuous improvement** represented both in the backlogs (i.e. improvements in deliverables) and in the retrospectives (i.e. process improvements), including the application of resulting process improvements *across* Agile project teams.

One final note regarding CMMI® and Agile: The natural convergence of these approaches is expected to emerge as Agile practitioners become more influential in management decisions:

"We are starting to see collisions as the younger folks who practice Agile in an organic manner start to move up in their organizations."[54]

This means that forward-thinking managers are in a position to leverage the benefits of using CMMI® and Agile approaches in both the short- and long-term strategies of the organization by establishing structures that *anticipate* a shift in Agile support from grassroots to boardrooms.

---

[54] *CMMI® and Agile: Opposites Attract* (2009): *www.executivebrief.com/CMMI/agile-CMMI/*.

ITIL®

The Information Technology Infrastructure Library®
(ITIL®) provides best practice approaches to managing and
adapting IT services to meet the ongoing business
requirements of the organization. It is comprised of five key
areas:

- Service strategy
- Service design
- Service transition
- Service operation
- Continual service improvement.

At face value, ITIL® appears to be a highly regimented
framework that aligns more closely with traditional
development methods, specifically with reference to
tightly-controlling change management processes. Changes
in the ITIL® framework are often implemented in a
"command and control" model, where agreed changes are
thrust upon the project team, instead of working
collaboratively with them to assess the impact of proposed
changes.[55]

The irony is that the "command and control" approach to
services management can actually *defeat* the primary
objective of ITIL®, which is to enhance IT services using
approaches that are:

- The most effective (to best support the business goals of
  the organization)

---

[55] *Agile Enterprise Administration: Beyond Data Administration*:
www.agiledata.org/essays/enterpriseAdministration.html.

- The least resource-intensive (to make the most efficient use of the available staff and budget)
- The least risky (to ensure continuity of service).

These objectives are at the very heart of the value that Agile approaches are designed to deliver.

The integration of ITIL® with Agile approaches does *not* negate the need for organizations to establish and utilize a change control team and change advisory board (CAB) to review the impact of proposed changes. An article by Pete Swabey – *Agile and ITIL® are Complementary Partners*[56] – specifically identifies the critical importance of the CAB and the change control team in maintaining the well-considered and well-paced delivery of the highest business-value changes for the organization.

In fact, the use of Agile methodologies to implement ITIL®-managed changes provides the organization with more frequent releases of fully functional, fully tested (and, for some organizations, continuously integrated) capabilities, which can significantly *mitigate* the risk of disruption to existing services.

There are current and emerging trends in the IT industry to support the combined use of ITIL® and Agile approaches, including: *service-oriented architectures (SOAs)*, which facilitate the incorporation of updated capabilities in

---

[56] *Agile and ITIL® are "complementary partners"*, Swabey P (2010): www.information-age.com/channels/management-and-skills/perspectives-and-trends/1149583/agile-and-ITIL-are-complementary-partners.thtml.

existing systems[57]; *DevOps*, where the project team and the customer (generally the operations staff) work collaboratively throughout the change management process; and *Lean-ITIL®*, which focuses on using Lean Development methodologies in the efficient implementation of approved changes (*see Lean Development in Chapter 4: Common Agile Methodologies at a Glance for further detail*).

Flexibility in ITIL®

As with the project and process frameworks described earlier in this chapter, each organization has the discretion to implement ITIL® in a way that supports Agile approaches, allowing the organization to receive frequent releases of the highest business-value changes. The core structures of ITIL® can incorporate Agile artifacts. For example, they can:

- Use a product backlog to record and prioritize requested enhancements and fixes, which can then serve as the forward schedule of changes (FSC) in support of the ITIL® model
- Use measurements that are tailored to the natural outputs of Agile work – including backlogs, burndown charts, work-in-progress charts and executive dashboards

where the artifacts selected are those that best align with the Agile approach(es) utilized by the organization.

---

[57] *Why ITIL® Service Management benefits from SOA and Agile methodologies*, McKendrick J (2010): *www.zdnet.com/blog/service-oriented/why-ITIL-service-management-benefits-from-soa-and-agile-methodologies/5738.*

13: Managing Agile within Your Existing Project Frameworks

Ideally, you can leverage your management position to persuade the organization to explicitly incorporate Agile approaches as an intrinsic part of the documented ITIL® planning, implementation and rollout processes. In reality, however, it may take some time for the organization to let go of the stringent "command and control" approaches in their current ITIL® processes – in which case, you may still find yourself facing the same challenges of trying to implement Agile approaches against big upfront specifications. Where the organization is unwilling to relinquish their existing practices, your team may be forced to use "Agile by stealth" to employ Agile practices as much as possible, with the understanding that a lack of organizational support for this can significantly diminish the overall value of the outcomes.

Quality management

Organizations generally implement a quality management system (QMS) for one of two primary reasons:

1. To provide a framework for improving the organization's business processes, generating higher-quality outputs, and increasing customer satisfaction, and/or
2. To meet industry, customer, contractual or procurement compliance requirements.

Similarly, if your organization has an established QMS, staff will generally fall into one of two distinct camps:

1. The people who adhere to QMS policies and procedures to the minimum level necessary for compliance (i.e. those who view QMS as a *burden*), or

2. The people who see your organization's QMS as a mechanism for encouraging standardized work practices in the organization to facilitate staff education, training, benchmarking, consistency of work, and higher-quality outputs (i.e. those who view QMS as an *opportunity*).

As an IT director, you are in a position to influence your staff to look at the organization's QMS framework as either a burden thrust upon them (e.g. by rolling your eyes when you hear about an upcoming audit), or as an opportunity to *critically review and improve* the work that they do. As the director of an *Agile* IT department, you have an even greater challenge of convincing teams who base their work on the principles of "just good enough" documentation that taking the time to contribute to, update and utilize QMS policy and procedure documentation is worth their time.

Agile work already has a number of mechanisms built into the methodologies and practices to promote and ensure the quality of outputs, including:

- Test-Driven Development
- Coding and modeling standards
- Pair programming
- Continuous integration
- Iterative reviews with the customer
- Retrospective reviews

in addition to a number of face-to-face communication channels that do not involve extensive documentation. These mechanisms are exceptionally good at ensuring that the team delivers high-quality outputs that align with the needs of the customer. What they generally lack, however, are mechanisms for adequately recording the Agile practices that are used by the team in a way that facilitates staff education, new hire training, outsourcing of development work, and new project start-up[58].

Integrating Agile work in your organization's QMS can be achieved by structuring QMS policies and procedures to identify Agile methodologies and practices as an accepted – or even preferred – method for software and services delivery in the organization.[59] This can serve as an opportunity for your staff to:

- Critically review the Agile methodologies and practices within and across their projects
- Establish a more consistent, clearly described and replicable model that can be used by other project teams, for training new hires, and for educating partner organizations.

Documenting these practices can also serve other business interests in the organization, including allowing the sales and marketing teams to more easily (and correctly) describe Agile practices to clients when they are promoting your IT services; allowing a consistent description of these practices to be included in proposals, tender responses, and contracts; as well as providing a benchmarking structure for QMS audit activities.

---

[58] There are noted exceptions to this, for example, the "Agile cookbook" developed by BT, which was deliberately written to educate staff on Agile practices and to promote consistency across the organization.
[59] *ISO 9001 and Agile Development* (2007): *http://agile2007.agilealliance.org/downloads/proceedings/055_ISO%209001_833.pdf*

Flexibility in QMS

QMS certification standards (e.g. ISO9001) are designed to be applicable to organizations of every size, in every industry, and across a broad range of business activities. They are, therefore, by necessity, structured to be high-level enough to give organizations the flexibility to adapt their QMS implementation to the specific needs of their business, as long as they meet the basic requirements for documentation, accountability, traceability and measurement. This means that, more than any other framework described in this chapter, the QMS policies and procedures in your organization can be adapted to incorporate Agile methodologies and practices as organizational standards.

Once Agile practices have been incorporated into your organization's QMS (and, ideally, you have documented your Agile practices to meet the organizational standards), audits of Agile work can then be based upon:

- Comparison of the team's day-to-day work against documented Agile practices
- Review of the measurements that are the natural outputs of Agile work (e.g. backlogs, burndown charts and executive dashboards)
- Review of defects through the artifacts that the Agile teams already produce (e.g. automated testing logs and issues lists)
- Review of the documented outcomes from iterative review sessions with the customer (or even the auditor's attendance at these sessions), combined with interviewing your customers.

This means that QMS compliance can be achieved with minimal additional overhead for your staff. With the right management direction, QMS policies and procedures can also provide your staff with the opportunity to regularly review and refine the Agile practices across all of their projects, and an even greater opportunity for the organization to consistently implement Agile practices more broadly.

Other frameworks

The project management, process improvement and quality management frameworks described in this chapter represent industry standard approaches that have been adopted across a number of organizations. The reality is, however, that the frameworks used in your organization may actually be a variation on one of these approaches, adapted to suit the constraints of your industry, the specialist nature of your work, or to align with other corporate management and compliance requirements. Alternatively, your organization may adhere to a project management or process improvement model that varies significantly from these frameworks.

If this is the case, the specific guidelines offered in the previous chapters may not directly apply to the structures that your organization works within; however, with some creative thinking, most of these frameworks can be positioned to align with Agile work.

If your organization uses a variation on (or a completely different model from) these standard frameworks, you will need to ask the following questions:

- How are the objectives and deliverables of each project defined? Can project initiation documents be abstracted to represent *strategic outcomes* instead of tactical ones? Will the project authority support an approach that identifies, communicates and confirms detailed deliverables as the project progresses?
- What are the primary drivers for established deadlines within the project? Is there any flexibility for the project team to have input into these timeframes, or are they always top-down directives? Are specific project outcomes tied to fixed delivery dates, or are deadlines based more on establishing an end date for project funding and resource allocation?
- Similarly, what are the drivers for project funding? Is it a fixed amount identified at the beginning of the project, or can it be adapted to suit emerging needs as the project progresses? (As Agile approaches focus on delivering the highest business-value features as early as possible, adapting budgets can often involve *scaling down* the initially allocated funding because project objectives have been achieved earlier than expected.)

The critical challenge for you is aligning the primary objectives of your organization's frameworks (e.g. budget management, revenue generation, risk management, resource planning, fulfilling contractual obligations, complying with regulatory requirements, and meeting shareholder demands) to the inherent benefits that are delivered through Agile work.

It should be noted that the introduction of an alternative framework does not magically remove the impediments of an organizational culture that has been built on centralized management control and a lack of trust in the project team. The only thing that is likely to remove these impediments (and pave the way for using Agile on future projects) is a proven track record of successful Agile projects (*see Chapter 8: Delivering Agile*).

If your organization uses such prescriptive and immovable frameworks that there is no flexibility to incorporate any of the above allowances to suit Agile work, you may need to resort to the high-overhead "Agile by stealth" approach described earlier in this chapter. This is not a preferred outcome, but at least it allows your staff to continue to utilize selected Agile practices without contravening corporate guidelines. Ideally, once you have a few successful Agile projects in your arsenal, decision makers will be more willing to consider adapting these frameworks to accommodate Agile work.

The bottom line

There is nothing to stop your organization from using Agile methodologies and practices as the tactical approach for delivering results within the structure and constraints of the project management, process improvement or quality management frameworks in your organization. This chapter has focused on defining (and re-defining) these frameworks to allow Agile approaches to be used as an intrinsic part of the standardized processes in your organization. It has also identified that compliance with organizational frameworks can be a much more manageable task when the organization appreciates the benefits that Agile approaches provide. Therefore, as a director, it is in your best interest to effectively communicate the core benefits of Agile (as described in *Chapter 3*) to those who are responsible for the frameworks in your organization. With their support, the alignment between Agile and existing frameworks can be achieved with significantly fewer overheads for your department.

CHAPTER 14: BUDGETING FOR AGILE WORK

Most Agile initiatives will be constrained by a budget allocation that is identified at the start of the process. Whether or not the budget is realistic, this is the amount available for the Agile team to use. So, it is critical that the department endeavors to maximize the business value that can be delivered within this constraint.

The following presents two ideal models for managing funding for Agile work, and then identifies how departments can realistically manage their budgets when the flexibility of the Agile-specific funding model is not possible.

The ideal

In an ideal world, budget allocations for Agile work would be managed using one of two models:

1. Per iteration cost, or
2. Per units of work cost

both of which are directly aligned with the incremental planning approaches used in Agile work. Each of these models is described in the following sections.

Management by iteration cost

Management by iteration cost effectively means that the department manages each initiative by allocating a team of resources (with an associated cost) for as many iterations as can be funded within the available budget. The determination of what work is undertaken by the team in each iteration (i.e. what high-priority features are delivered) is left to the joint decision of the customer and the project team as part of the planning work for each iteration. Each iteration planning session also provides the opportunity (where needed) for the department to compare the business value of remaining work for that initiative against the cost of future iterations, in order to determine whether available resources could be more effectively assigned to other high-value activities in the department.

In order to calculate per iteration budgeting costs, you need to:

- Determine the per iteration cost of the resources on the project team using the standard full-time equivalent (FTE) calculations in your organization for the two- to four-week period. This is the *project team cost*[60]
- Identify any additional overhead costs that are known upfront, such as equipment that needs to be purchased or facilities that need to be acquired. This is the *known overhead cost*.

Then use the formula in *Figure 5* to determine how much work can be achieved (the number of iterations remaining) within the allocated budget for that initiative:

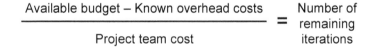

$$\frac{\text{Available budget} - \text{Known overhead costs}}{\text{Project team cost}} = \begin{array}{l}\text{Number of} \\ \text{remaining} \\ \text{iterations}\end{array}$$

Figure 5: Budgeting per iteration formula

---

[60] Note that some organizations also include the cost of the customer's time for iteration planning and outcomes review work in these calculations.

The number of remaining iterations identifies the duration of future work that the team can commit to within the initially allocated available budget.

At each iteration planning session, the customer and the project team are in a position to revisit this calculation using the information available at that time, specifically:

- The remaining available budget
- Any additional known overhead costs (e.g. equipment that is now needed based on a newly identified requirement)
- Any changes to resourcing levels in the team.

Running this same calculation at each iteration-planning session will allow the department to know how many more iterations are remaining within the available budget – and, most importantly, it will enable the customer to calculate the business value of the remaining work against that figure. This will help identify whether the value of proposed work aligns with the cost of subsequent iterations, which can help the department to determine the extent to which the initiative should continue.

From a budget-management perspective, this is the absolute simplest way to manage expended and ongoing costs for an Agile initiative. It does, however, require a level of trust in the Agile approach (and in the project team) to deliver business value without committing to a predetermined set of features for the allocated funds. Therefore, it is more likely to be applicable to Agile work with a longstanding customer.

Management by units of work

In situations where the department (or the customer) wants to directly correlate budget expenditure with the *specific features* of the solution that will be delivered within the allocated funding, the *management by units of work* model can be used to determine the budget dollars needed to support this work.

The "management by units of work" model assigns a number of units to each feature in the backlog item, based on the *expected effort* needed for the team to deliver that feature (e.g. one for simple features, five for complex features). The sum of all the assigned units of work across all of the features scheduled for an iteration, a release, or even the project overall, can then be combined with information on the team's historical rate of delivery (i.e. their velocity) for equivalent projects to determine how long the project team will need to deliver the features.

In order to calculate "units of work" budgeting costs for an entire project, you need to:

• Have the project team allocate a number of units to each item (i.e. feature) on the requirements backlog. This is the **item effort.**

• Calculate the *total item effort* for all the backlog items that are scheduled to be delivered for the entire project. This is the **project effort.**

• Use the team's historical velocity to identify how many units (on average) they are able to deliver per iteration, noting that the work should be of an equivalent complexity[61]. This is the ***team delivery rate.***

- Determine the per iteration cost of the resources on the project team using the standard full-time equivalent (FTE) calculations in your organization for the two- to four-week period. This is the ***project team cost.***

- Identify any additional overhead costs that are known upfront, such as equipment that needs to be purchased or facilities that need to be acquired. This is the ***known overhead cost.***

Then use the formula in *Figure 6* to determine how much budget allocation is required to deliver the full scope of project work:

$$\left(\frac{\text{Project effort}}{\text{Team delivery rate}} \times \begin{array}{c}\text{Project team}\\\text{cost}\end{array} \right) + \begin{array}{c}\text{Known}\\\text{overhead}\\\text{costs}\end{array} = \begin{array}{c}\text{Budget}\\\text{required}\end{array}$$

Figure 6: Budgeting per units of work formula

Using this model, you can also calculate the required budget allocation for all of the features in a planned iteration or release. This means that an equivalent approach to *management by iteration cost* can be used to estimate the cost of delivering the remaining items in the backlog at

---

[61] Where the team is newly formed – or the budgeted work is significantly different from previous projects – you may need to estimate this number until the team has established a reliable velocity.

each iteration planning session – and to make subsequent decisions on the best overall use of the department's resources.

As with all estimation work, using the team's velocity to calculate productivity rates is not an exact science. Other unforeseen variables (e.g. sick leave) could impact the team's future productivity levels – or the scheduled work may be more (or less) complex than was originally envisaged. It is, however, a way for you to know reasonably well where to "draw the line" on future backlog work, which will assist you in future budget planning.

The reality

Although budget management for Agile work is ideally structured using one of the models described in the previous section, the reality is that you are probably working with a fixed budget allocation that is tied to:

- An immovable deadline, and/or
- A pre-determined scope of work.

If you are planning to use Agile approaches to deliver these requirements, then you may need to retrofit your iterative work into these fixed constraints using a variation on the *management by iteration cost* model that was described in the previous section, as described below:

- Determine how many iterations of work your staff can do by:
  - Using the formula in *Figure 5* to identify the number of remaining iterations within the available budget

o Using the immovable deadline to determine how many iterations can be completed in the available time.

• Work with the customer to ensure that the items at the top of the backlog correspond to the pre-determined scope for this work (or that they actively agree to a variation on this scope).

There will, inevitably, be differences in the number of iterations of work for the remaining budget, the remaining time, and the remaining work to be completed. If there is more available budget than time, you can supplement the project team (or establish a second, concurrent team), so that more capability is delivered. However, if there is more available time than budget, you will need to put an end date on internal work, even if that date is before the agreed deadline.

The bottom line

Working within a fixed budget amount may mean that there are insufficient funds to achieve everything that the organization would like (as is generally the case with budget allocations). Unlike traditional software development methods, however, the very nature of Agile approaches can guarantee that the limited budget available will not be squandered on work that brings little value to the organization.

CHAPTER 15: REPORTING ON AGILE PROJECTS

Monitoring the business value and progress of the Agile work in your department can begin from the moment each project starts, and continue well before the whole-of-life business value of the overall initiative is evident. As described in *Chapter 10: Using Agile Tools* and *Chapter 11: Measuring Agile Success,* Agile approaches provide a number of mechanisms for tracking progress, which include formal reports (e.g. executive dashboards), status update tools (e.g. WIP boards and product backlogs), and ongoing communication with stakeholders. Arguably, however, the most valuable measure of the Agile team's progress is their delivery of *tangible outputs.* For iterative Agile methodologies, such as Scrum and FDD™, the presentation of working software occurs at the end of each iteration. This means that, at fixed timeframes (generally once a month), you are able to see firsthand whether these approaches are delivering their agreed outcomes (i.e. business value).

Equally important, the project teams themselves are able to use these Agile tools to monitor their own progress during each iteration, and to adjust their ongoing work as needed to meet their agreed commitments.

This positions Agile reporting as an intrinsic tool that enables staff to *monitor* and *self-manage* their work – identifying and addressing issues that impede their progress – not an added overhead that distracts them from delivering value to the organization.

The ideal

The ideal Agile reporting environment would leverage the tools described in *Chapter 10: Using Agile Tools* without asking staff to do extra (often redundant) work to meet corporate reporting requirements. Specifically, this would involve using:

• Executive dashboards to provide an overview of work completed and pending, budget utilization, resource utilization, and issues raised
• Backlogs, Kanban charts and other detailed progress-tracking tools for where management requires further information
• Communication methods – other than paper reporting – to provide an update on work progress, such as participation in daily stand-up meetings and iterative review sessions.

This ideal model means that Agile teams could continue to use the reporting tools that are a standard (and natural) part of their Agile work; and that corporate reporting would not be a separate overhead for staff that takes them away from their core work.

Equally, in this ideal model, management would be satisfied with keeping track of work progress through executive dashboards, with access to backlogs, Kanban charts, etc. – and even attending daily stand-up meetings or iterative review sessions – where more detail is required.

Detailed staff time-tracking would be less of a focus for the department than tracking the *productivity* of staff members. Therefore, timesheets would not be required in this model, as detailed information about resource allocations and work would be continually available to management through the backlogs.

Even in an ideal model, however, it is reasonable to expect that some level of budget management – and, therefore, budget reporting – will be needed by the department. The Agile budgeting mechanisms described in *Chapter 14: Budgeting for Agile Work* would continue to provide the required levels of departmental budget tracking without creating unnecessary additional overheads for staff.

The reality

In most organizations, *every* department is required to provide consistent budget, resourcing, time tracking, work status, risks and issue details through a number of standard corporate reports. The IT department is no exception. Therefore, the following provides strategies for aligning your department's Agile work with the mandatory corporate reporting structures in your organization.

Aligning Agile work with reporting cycles

The most efficient way to incorporate Agile work into your overall departmental reporting requirements is to align iterative work to correspond with your standard reporting cycles.

If your department is required to provide corporate reporting on a *monthly* basis (e.g. on the last business day of each month), then the four-week iterations within an Agile project could be timed to correspond with this. This means that Agile teams could use the presentation of working software at the end of each iteration to report on their progress, in conjunction with the standard reporting cycles for the organization overall. The completion of each iteration would also provide you with the corresponding details on resource and budget utilization for the previous month, along with an up-to-date summary of work delivered, the project status and any outstanding issues during that iteration. Note that this information can also be extracted across multiple iterations, but it would be more time-consuming to isolate information, such as partially completed functionality or temporary issues that are expected to be resolved at the next iterative review session.

If your department is required to provide corporate reporting on a *quarterly* basis (i.e. every 13 weeks), then you can align the outcomes from three cumulative four-week (or six cumulative two-week) iterations to correspond with this cycle, with the potential for staff to utilize the remaining week in each quarter to assist in reporting, undertake training, or do other required departmental work[62].

Where the Agile work in your department is an ongoing process, *annual reporting* can be structured as the cumulative result of 12 four-week iterations within or across multiple projects. However, it is likely that you will need to combine the information gathered through Agile tools with the tracking tools used in the other traditional project work in your department to achieve this.

For departmental reporting that falls *within* iterations (e.g. weekly reporting or ad hoc reporting requests), the information tracked on a daily basis in the backlog tools –

---

[62] This quarterly reporting structure for Agile work was first introduced to me by Joseph Pelrine (*www.metaprog.com*).

and rolled into the executive dashboard – should provide you with the detail that you need to calculate the metrics. This information will not be as readily encapsulated as the results from a completed iteration, but it is likely to provide far more detail than the half-completed timesheets and quickly drafted status update e-mails that tend to be used for ad hoc reporting in traditional project environments.

Budget reporting

The budget-tracking measures identified in *Chapter 14: Budgeting for Agile Work* provide mechanisms for you to identify and track Agile project work against allocated budget dollars.

Executive dashboards and backlogs further allow you to identify the historical, current and planned utilization of resources on your Agile teams at any point in time. Where staff members are fully allocated to Agile work, these tools allow you to:

- Calculate the overall time that has been spent for each project across all resources
- Estimate the remaining resource time based on work allocated for subsequent iterations.

The irony is that most corporate budget reports focus exclusively on the *amount of money expended* by the project, not on the *business value generated* for that expenditure. With Agile tools, you actually have *more* information available for you to track your ROI than your organization is likely to require.

Resource and time tracking

If there is a standard time-tracking tool used by the organization, the members of the Agile team may have to do some redundant work to record their project work in the backlog, and then separately record their time in the corporate reporting tool. However, once there is a substantial enough commitment to Agile in your department (and a critical mass of your staff using these approaches), it may be valuable for you to consider having the team build an interface between your backlog tools and your time-tracking system, so that work on Agile projects is pre-populated into the timesheet. Staff may still need to supplement the pre-populated timesheet with the work done on traditional projects, other departmental work, corporate meetings, etc., but this should be minimal in comparison to separately recording *all* of their day-to-day work.

The bottom line

The more discretion that your department has to align Agile work with standard corporate reporting cycles, the easier it will be to allow the standard reporting tools used in Agile work to feed into your departmental reporting requirements.

It is important to note that Agile reporting tools gather most (if not all) of the detailed information needed as input into your departmental reporting. So, the challenge for you is not in getting staff to retrospectively fill in their timesheets, provide status updates on three-week-old work, or put together ad hoc estimates of their planned work; the challenge is in combining the more extensive detail from your Agile projects with the limited detail available from the traditional projects in your department.

CHAPTER 16: ESTABLISHING AGILE CONTRACTS

If you manage an IT department that develops software for external clients, you will find that establishing a contract that genuinely supports Agile approaches can be a significant challenge for your organization. By its very nature, a contract that specifies *detailed upfront deliverables* contravenes the principles of flexibility and adaptation that are at the heart of Agile approaches[63]. However, the actual problem is not the detail in a contract – it is the unspoken reason *why* the detail is there in the first place.

Although the detail in a contract is often mandated by compliance requirements, organizational standards and legal imperatives, underpinning this detail is a *lack of trust* in the relationship between the vendor and the client. By putting extensive detail into a software development agreement, the client is seeking protection from the risk of insufficient outcomes (or non-delivery of outcomes), budget overruns and missed deadlines. The more that this risk is perceived by the client, the more the contract will endeavor to mitigate the risk through an abundance of clauses to account for every possible contingency.

Agile takes a very different approach to working arrangements with clients. Instead of focusing on faults and liabilities, Agile approaches focus on *collaboration, transparency and trust*. The relationship between the client

---

[63] Similar to the issue with prescriptive project frameworks identified in *Chapter 13: Managing Agile Within Your Existing Project Frameworks.*

and the vendor is based on *shared goals, shared knowledge, shared risks and shared benefits*.

This section provides guidelines for establishing a mutually agreeable contract that supports Agile approaches – and, equally, for adapting existing contracts to allow Agile approaches to be used by your development staff.

The ideal

If you are in a position to control the content of your software development agreement, then there are four key elements to the ideal Agile contract:

1. **Deliverables are identified as *business objectives* that are *measurable*:** For example, "the solution will increase staff output by 30% within six months of its release." The words in italics are what differentiate Agile contract deliverables from those in standard software development agreements:

   * Identifying *business objectives* focuses the agreement on the bottom-line benefits that the solution needs to deliver to the organization, not the specific features of the delivered software. It allows the customer and the project team to work collaboratively to determine the best solution to achieve the stated objective – and, most importantly, it provides the team with flexibility to adapt the solution as new technical, organizational and market information emerges.

   * Working with *measurable* deliverables assures the client that determining the successful fulfillment of the contract work will not be left to the discretion of any one party. The measurable results can be based on quantifiable KPIs (such as the revenue generated

or the operational cost savings) and/or qualitative measures (such as surveys that measure user satisfaction). The critical component is identifying the measures of success upfront, and keeping these goals at the forefront of the minds of the project team as work is undertaken.

2. **The *process* is detailed, not the solution:** Instead of providing extensive upfront detail on the solution that is the work product of the contract, focus on describing the *process* that will be used to ensure that the work product achieves the client's objectives. The contract should explicitly identify that the vendor and client will jointly follow the Agile processes of working collaboratively, focusing on the highest business-value capabilities as defined by the customer, and adjusting ongoing work based on the customer's regular review of delivered outputs. The process described in the contract should also identify the Agile communication channels that will be in place, and how the status of ongoing development work will be shared with the client. Note that, if your department has integrated Agile work into the organization's QMS documentation, the details describing your Agile processes may already be available for use in these contracts.

3. **Pricing is structured by *iteration*:** Most standard IT contracts structure payment milestones around:
   • The completion of software development life cycle (SDLC) phases (e.g. 20% upon completion of requirements analysis, 30% upon completion of acceptance testing), or

- Around the acceptance of pre-defined deliverables (such as 40% for the data entry screens, 30% for the automated reports).

As Agile work is designed to complete the full SDLC for the subset of capabilities being delivered *in each iteration* – and as the use of pre-defined deliverables defeats the very purpose of Agile approaches – the ideal Agile contract should structure payment milestones around the completion of work per iteration. This allows the client to tie payments to delivered business value without constraining the work to fit within a prescribed traditional IT payment model. As indicated in *Chapter 14: Budgeting for Agile Work*, the total value of the contract can be subdivided into an agreed number of iterations, with payment tied to the completion of specified iterations (i.e. one four-week iteration for monthly payments, three four-week iterations for quarterly payments).

4. *Flexibility* **is built in where possible:** Although contracts generally require enough structure to be enforceable agreements, there should be sufficient flexibility built into the contract terms to allow for *agreed* variations on:
   - Deliverables
   - Costs
   - Delivery dates, and
   - Status reporting mechanisms
   so that the agreed Agile approach is not unduly constrained by predefined contract terms that contravene the process; for example, it is important to keep flexibility to adjust delivery dates to correspond with the

client's decision to release a subset of high-priority functionality.

It is important to note that the "ideal" Agile contract structure *does not* negate the need for organizations to apply due diligence in their agreements by including standard contract terms and conditions. Termination clauses, payment terms, confidentiality clauses, intellectual property terms, etc. are all necessary to protect the interest of the involved parties. The primary difference between a traditional contract and an Agile one is that the Agile contract stipulates a *process* for achieving successful outcomes, whereas the traditional contract handcuffs the parties to a level of predetermined detail that virtually assures that the eventual outcomes will be inadequate or obsolete.

The reality

Although having a contract that reasonably accommodates Agile work is the ideal, it is also a relatively rare occurrence in the IT industry. Most IT contracts are structured around traditional project approaches, with pre-defined scopes, budgets and timelines; and very few of these contracts provide sufficient flexibility to allow for mutually agreed alternative approaches to be used.

If you have already signed – or are about to sign – a traditional IT project contract, the first thing that you will need to do is check for where the contract allows for acceptable variations, such as mutually agreed amendments to contract terms, or terms in the attachments (e.g. work orders) superseding terms in the contract body. If the contract does allow for variations, then the challenge for you will be to sell to the client the benefits of Agile approaches in order to amend the existing contract – or to structure the new contract so that it allows for this flexibility. (As a last resort, you could propose to the client that the current inflexible contract be terminated and replaced altogether, but it is extremely unlikely that a client would be willing to do that!)

The reality is that you will most likely be retrofitting your Agile work into a less-than-Agile contract; in which case, the following guidelines may assist you in overcoming this challenge:

- If the contract has specified *delivery date(s)*, ensure that Agile work outputs are aligned to these timeframes, even if one final date in the contract actually represents multiple iterative deliverables.
- If the contract has specified *costs*, structure your Agile teams and iterations to work within the allocated budget, as identified in *Chapter 14: Budgeting for Agile Work*. Ideally, you can negotiate with the client to prioritize and scope work to fit within a specified number of iterations.
- If the contract has a specified *scope*, particularly one defined at a detailed level, you will need to work with the client on the best way for you to *jointly* address this constraint. If the client is truly aware of the benefits of Agile approaches, they will appreciate that this constraint is actually limiting *their* flexibility to respond to the capabilities that your team delivers. If you have the client on board, there are a few ways to address the pre-defined scope constraint, including:
  - Agreeing with the client to establish functionality trade-offs, where higher-priority capabilities that

emerge from Agile processes are delivered in lieu of selected capabilities that were listed in the original contract

o Agreeing with the client to redefine the pre-defined scope to be more high-level (i.e. based on strategic outcomes), with flexibility for the details of the deliverables to evolve as work progresses

o Amending the contract to describe the detailed scope as "indicative" capabilities, with reference to final delivered capabilities as agreed with the client.

Although fitting Agile work in a traditional contract can be frustrating, it can also be an opportunity for you to introduce clients to the benefits of using Agile approaches for work that was originally structured around a traditional project approach. Over time, a client who becomes more comfortable with the value of Agile approaches may be willing to accommodate more flexible arrangements in future contracts.

The bottom line

Agile work can absolutely be undertaken within contractually driven time, budgetary and scope constraints. Whether you have the flexibility to structure an "ideal Agile contract" or you are working within a more traditional contract arrangement, the key is to retrofit the Agile work to meet whatever constraints are defined in the contract – not to forego the opportunity to use Agile approaches due to the contract restrictions.

Inevitably, there will be situations in which an existing contract is defined with extensively detailed capabilities, and with no flexibility to adjust work as it progresses. If the client cannot be persuaded by the benefits of Agile approaches – and if they are genuinely unwilling to consider provisions that allow these approaches to be used in the project work – then you may have to make the decision to use selected Agile practices internally (such as daily stand-up meetings, so that your team can at least benefit from working in a high-communication environment). Alternatively, you could take a calculated risk of using Agile approaches *regardless* of what the contract stipulates, in the hope that, once the client sees the benefits of these approaches, they will be willing to consider amending the contract. In this situation, however, it may be best for you to relegate this project to traditional methods, and focus your efforts on negotiating Agile work with other clients.

CHAPTER 17: BUILDING THE RIGHT AGILE TEAM

Putting together a successful Agile project team has as much to do with finding the right mix of technical skills as it has to do with finding the right *team dynamic*.

Agile work requires team members to be:

*   **Multi-skilled**, so that they are *able* to take on the variety of roles that may be needed by the team as work progresses
*   **Open-minded and flexible**, so that they are *willing* to take on the necessary roles
*   **Highly communicative**, to encourage an environment of idea sharing, joint development, and collaborative issue resolution
*   **Self-motivated**, so that they can work independently as well as working with the other members of the team
*   **Holistic thinkers**, so that they can appreciate both the technical and the business context of the work that they are doing.

The regular delivery of fully functional, fully tested capabilities that align with customer priorities requires a *multidisciplinary* project team, where team members are as comfortable discussing business requirements with the customer as they are designing the solution, building the test cases, coding the features, and writing online help manuals for the users. This does not mean that every member of the team needs to be a skilled programmer, but it *does* mean that every skilled programmer on the team needs to be willing to be a part-time business analyst, part-time tester and part-time technical writer.

One of the most fascinating elements of strong Agile teams is their ability to apply *natural skills and strengths compensation* in their work. Because successful delivery is the responsibility of the team as a whole, strong Agile teams will naturally "divide and conquer" the work required based on the relative skills, strengths and availability of each team member. They avoid pigeonholing themselves into exclusive roles in favor of doing *whatever the team needs* in order to get the job done. They also trust their other team members to do the same.

This means that, although technical skills are important to ensure that required work can be done, Agile approaches do not require every member of the team to be the world's greatest programmer. In fact, they require the exact opposite.

The ideal

In an ideal world, you would have Agile teams of four to eight people, each of whom is able – and willing – to take on *any* role required by the team at any time. In addition, the team members will have worked with Agile approaches – and with each other – in the past, so that there is a short learning curve to get them started, and a history of their velocity (i.e. their rates of productivity) as a team so that you can accurately estimate ongoing work.

Although this is a realistic model to aim for in your department a year or two down the track, in the short-term, it would be beneficial for you to put together a project team that either has:

- A strong existing team dynamic, from having worked together on other projects before, or
- People with the right mix of communication skills, flexibility and self-motivation to build that strong dynamic.

It would be beneficial for a few of the team members to have had exposure to Agile approaches in the past, but this is absolutely not the most important characteristic. Agile methodologies and practices can be learned; collaboration, trust, communication and teamwork are far more difficult attributes to instill in your staff.

For team members who have traditionally taken on one specific role in the software development life cycle, this is the opportunity to explain that Agile work requires each team member to take on whatever role is needed throughout the project (within reason).

For example, iterative software development methodologies, such as Scrum and FDD™, stipulate that the team must produce *tested, working software*, which means that developers should be prepared to equally act as business analysts, testers or technical writers if that is the most critical work that the project needs.

Realistically, not every Agile team member will be able to take on every other role in the team. For example, a software tester may not have the skills to do programming work, but they should be more than capable of writing user guides for the software that they test, or working with the users to determine how a new feature should behave. Not only does multidisciplinary work enable the team to focus their efforts on the most urgent needs of the project, it also gives them experience with (and empathy for) the work that their other team members are doing.

The reality

You already have existing staff in your IT department, and there is little (to no) budget available to hire additional dedicated resources for Agile projects[64]. Most likely, your IT department is comprised of a variety of specialist resources, including software developers, systems and database administrators, testers, business analysts and technical writers. Generally, each team member has been pigeonholed on previous software development projects into the role defined in their official job title; and they are quite comfortable staying in that role.

If you work in a relatively small (or particularly enlightened) IT department, however, many of these resources will have had the opportunity – or the necessity – to take on multiple hats in their previous projects. If so, you are already several steps ahead of the game, because your staff are likely to already be comfortable with changing roles to suit the needs of the project (and flexible enough to work in this model). If not, this is where you want to start.

Chapter 8: Delivering Agile recommended that your department begins Agile work by taking on a small, but meaningful project where your selected Agile approaches will be used (your "Agile trial project"). Not only does this give your team an opportunity to become familiar with Agile principles and practices, it also gives them the

---

[64] Let alone any budget to hire an expert consultant to guide your team in their transition to Agile work.

confidence to take on a new approach in their work without feeling as though they are being indefinitely thrust into a changed work environment. For most staff with trepidations, simply having the opportunity to trial Agile approaches on one project will be enough to give them the confidence to continue using these approaches for additional work.

Once you have identified the team that will be assigned to the Agile trial project, the first thing you will need to do is introduce this team to the *principles* that underpin Agile (no matter which Agile approaches your department intends to use). This introduction should focus on the key characteristics that differentiate Agile from traditional software development approaches.

Then, you should try to encourage each team member to *actively participate* in the iteration planning work, discussing business requirements with the customer, translating the items in the requirements backlog into technical tasks in the delivery backlog, and working with the other members of the project team on realistic estimates for the required work.

Once work has begun, you can facilitate the team's introduction to Agile approaches by encouraging them to divide tasks between themselves, so that everyone on the team has a reasonable opportunity to try out different roles. You should also facilitate the first few iteration review sessions, encouraging each team member to actively work with the customer. Although Agile teams are meant to be self-motivated and independent, they may need your assistance in the transition.

In choosing the team members for the trial Agile project, you also need to be careful not to pigeonhole staff yourself, based on your experience with them in traditional software projects. If a programmer in your department has a reputation for being a loner, this could be the result of years of working virtually independently on software projects, not an inherent weakness in their character. Give programmers a chance to work with an Agile team (or two). They may surprise you and step up to the challenge – or they may recede even further into their shells. If all else fails, you can keep them on traditional software development projects and assign future Agile work to other staff who are more comfortable working in a collaborative environment.

Also, do not be afraid to think beyond the traditional IT roles; someone who is naturally inclined to work with business users could become an excellent customer representative (or take on more business analysis work for the team), even if their prior background has been more technical. This opportunity could also expose them to other people's perspectives, which could significantly improve the quality and relevance of their development work.

The bottom line

Whether you are in a position to hand-pick flexible, highly communicative team players to staff your Agile projects – or you are working with a mix of these skills in existing employees – the best way to progress your Agile work is to set the stage with a strong foundation of core Agile principles, methodologies and practices, and with opportunities for the team to provide you with frequent feedback. Most importantly, you will demonstrate your flexibility as a manager to adjust Agile work as it progresses to best suit the need of your teams. This may include changing the duration of iterations to align with team preferences, reassigning staff who are genuinely not comfortable with these approaches, or even acting as a team member yourself to facilitate the close work with the business areas. Agile purists may balk at the idea of changing team members or the duration of each iteration "in flight" (as this minimizes your ability to accurately track team velocity); but, in order for Agile approaches to genuinely work in your department, you need to find the dynamic that works best for you and your staff.

CHAPTER 18: CONDUCTING PERFORMANCE REVIEWS FOR AGILE TEAMS

Understanding the best way to structure performance reviews for Agile teams requires a quick look back at *why* organizations conduct performance reviews in the first place.

Beyond the human resources mandate that performance reviews must be conducted for each member of your staff, is the opportunity for these reviews to:

* Acknowledge the positive contributions that the employee has made to the organization
* Identify and address potential areas for improvement
* Reward the employee, based on their performance (e.g. give merit-based bonuses)
* Encourage employee feedback on management and/or the organization overall
* Be documented for recordkeeping, reference and legal purposes.

In effect, a performance review is a "status report" for the employee: a summary produced at time-based intervals (e.g. quarterly or annually) that is intended to ensure due diligence on the part of the department. This means that the same issues that occur when the progress of a project is measured exclusively through status reports[65] equally occur when the progress of an employee is measured through performance reports.

---

[65] *See Chapter 11: Measuring Agile Success.*

The Agile world takes a completely different perspective on performance reviews. In the same way that Agile approaches measure progress through *tangible results*, they also use tangible results to monitor the team's performance. If the team is producing high-value solutions, this will be evident (and acknowledged) in the iteration review sessions. Conversely, if the team is *not* producing the expected level of value or quality, this will also be evident in the iteration review sessions – and addressed further in the retrospective. This means that, at least one time during each iteration, team members will get direct feedback from the customer on the work that they are doing – and the opportunity to address (and resolve) issues in their performance.

The challenge, of course, is that Agile work is undertaken by a *team of people,* whereas performance reviews are generally intended for *one employee.* So, how do you reconcile approaches that encourage teamwork and collaboration with performance review structures that reward individual achievements?

The ideal

In an ideal world, formal performance reviews would be replaced with the regular review of outputs, ongoing team communication and retrospective reviews that occur naturally in Agile work. Performance would be measured – and rewarded – at a team level, not for each individual. Salary reviews would be undertaken for the team as a whole, with each team member getting an equivalent percentage increase based on the performance of the team as a whole.

Part of this ideal model would empower the team to be self-managing in reviewing the performance of other team members. If there were issues with the performance of individual employees, these would first be addressed by the team itself, with the involvement of management only where needed. This would enable the team to genuinely succeed as a whole, without a subset of team members doing an unequal amount of the work.

In addition to reporting on progress through Agile tools, iteration review sessions and retrospectives, the team would be responsible for regularly communicating with management on a range of issues, including team performance and alignment with departmental expectations. This would also be the opportunity for the team to provide feedback on management and/or the organization overall.

If the organization required documented evidence to show that performance reviews have occurred, this could be developed as part of the standard reporting cycle for the department (*see Chapter 15: Reporting on Agile Projects*), with the natural outputs of Agile work (e.g. backlogs) being used as evidence to support the team's performance over the specified timeframe.

The reality

The reality is that most organizations cannot support a structure where performance reviews are undertaken by team, and not by individual employee. (Arguably, most employees would also be uncomfortable with this structure at first.)

It would also be unlikely that the human resources department would be willing to forego their standard performance review paperwork in favor of getting product backlogs and customer testimonials instead.

This means that you can use Agile tools as input into assessing the performance of the team, but you will almost inevitably need to conduct formal performance reviews with the team members individually.

The bottom line

Approaches that genuinely encourage and reward teamwork do not naturally align with organizational structures that encourage and reward individuals. Performance reviews – such as upfront budget planning and monthly corporate status reporting – are artifacts of a traditional organizational structure that Agile approaches are likely to supplement, not replace.

On a more positive note, however, both you and the employee do not need to wait until the end of each quarter – or each year – to actively assess the work that they are doing. Performance reviews are just a formal way of documenting the results that you are already seeing and communicating throughout the course of each Agile project.

CHAPTER 19: AVOIDING COMMON AGILE TRAPS

The simplicity and low overheads that make using Agile methodologies so appealing also make it highly susceptible to misapplication. The following identifies some of the most common traps that organizations have fallen into when implementing Agile.

Undermining Agile principles

There is a difference between adapting Agile to suit the preferred work practices of your organization (e.g. adjusting iteration timeframes or using videoconferencing instead of face-to-face meetings), and adapting Agile in a way that *contravenes* the underlying principles that drive its effectiveness. For example, applying a handful of Agile practices (e.g. daily stand-up meetings and Test-Driven Development) *without* the benefit of the core elements of each Agile methodology, such as stakeholder confirmation of requirements, or the ongoing adjustment of work to accommodate emerging information. In the Agile methodologies selection workflow tool, it was identified that, for projects without stakeholder availability, the use of selected Agile practices may be the only option available for the project team. In this situation, however, the outcome will be a somewhat more efficient traditional software development process – *not* an Agile project.

Insufficient communication and/or training

In order for Agile to be effective, participants (customers, managers and project team members) need to be educated on the principles and practices of the selected methodologies. Otherwise, they (and the organization) are likely to fall victim to the areas of misapplication identified in the previous section.

When introducing Agile in your department, it is important to consider how Agile principles and practices will be communicated to staff. Previously, it was identified that a cost-effective way to achieve this is by including an Agile resources page on your corporate intranet that provides links to relevant sites and allows staff to exchange their questions, concerns and ideas about the use of the methodologies before work begins.

Alternatively, your department may benefit from more formal guidance on adopting and applying Agile methodologies. There are a number of formal training courses available to teach people how to more effectively apply Agile methodologies. In some cases (e.g. Scrum) there are even formal certification courses that staff can attend.

All of these communication approaches will help to assure you that selected Agile methodologies are being implemented properly, and to the greatest advantage of the department.

Using Agile as a doctrine instead of a tool

This last common area of misapplication is following Agile as a strict doctrine without adapting it to the specific needs of your department. To receive the greatest benefit from using Agile methodologies, it is important to allow your staff to adjust and modify them in a way that fits in with their preferred work practices, as well as the department overall. That is, as long as the underlying principles of Agile are not compromised.

However you and your staff choose to introduce Agile within your department, you can (and should) adapt it to suit your specific needs. By its very nature, Agile methodologies are meant to be, well, agile.

CHAPTER 20: EXPANDING AGILE[66]

After your department has had the opportunity to trial Agile methodologies for a few months, it would be valuable for you to step back and ask yourself the following questions:

* Are teams delivering high business-value solutions within available budgets?
* Are the stakeholders getting the outcomes that they need?
* Are staff members happier to be working in a high-communication environment, rather than in a documentation-centric one?
* Is the quality of their work better than before?

The answers to these questions should provide you with sufficient information to consider broadening the use of Agile methodologies to other projects in your department. (Or, conversely, to decide that Agile methodologies are not suited to your department and should not be extended further; in which case, the low start-up costs of Agile have enabled you to make that decision without foregoing a huge upfront investment.)

One of the greatest advantages of Agile is that, in the same way that these approaches protect the organization from the risk of large upfront commitments, they also do not require

---

[66] Several of the strategies identified for expanding Agile work have been adapted from the equivalent sections in *Agile Productivity Unleashed: Proven Approaches for Achieving Real Productivity Gains in Any Organization*, Jamie Lynn Cooke, IT Governance Publishing (2010) and *Agile: An Executive Guide – Real results from IT budgets*, Jamie Lynn Cooke, IT Governance Publishing (2011).

a large upfront commitment from the organization in order to be used. Agile approaches are not highly regimented management structures that require hundreds of staff to attend workshops (and receive doorstops of documentation) before they can be used in the organization. Other areas can immediately apply many of the core Agile approaches (and principles) described in this book without attending week-long training courses, acquiring mounds of manuals, or enlisting the services of high-end consulting firms.

This means that using Agile approaches can be a cost-effective, low-risk option for other areas in the organization to trial.

So, if you decide to expand the use of Agile methodologies to other areas within (or outside of) your department, the next step will be to establish a strategy for *broadening awareness* of the value of Agile methodologies – and for encouraging other areas to trial them.

This strategy should include four key elements:

1. **Information:** educating staff on the quantitative and qualitative business value of Agile methodologies. This can be done through:
   - Internal "road show" events to show people the tangible outcomes from your Agile work
   - Putting materials on your corporate intranet, including the details in *Chapter 3: The Core Business Benefits of Agile*
   - Documenting the outcomes of your trial project(s) as a case study for other teams.
2. **Motivation:** using the information above, along with your influence, to encourage specific people to trial

Agile methodologies in their areas (e.g. those who are more open to trying new approaches, or those who have had historical problems with their software development projects)

3. **Selection:** helping interested teams to select the Agile methodology(ies) that are best suited to their activities (using your experience, along with the tools provided in *Chapter 9: Selecting the Right Agile Approach for Your Needs*)

4. **Collaboration:** providing assistance (and, where appropriate, experienced Agile team members) to help each area in their initial application of Agile methodologies. This includes educating the area on the principles and practices of their selected Agile methodology via:
   * An easy-to-use guide that explains the basics of Agile methodologies (such as the "Agile Cookbook" that was created by BT)
   * Internal training sessions to walk through and demonstrate the methodologies
   * Industry resources, such as those listed in *Chapter 21: More Information on Agile.*

You may also choose to position yourself as an Agile champion within the organization, using industry case studies (such as Microsoft and Yahoo!) and industry research (such as that by Forrester and VersionOne) to support your decision to trial Agile methodologies. Your experience with Agile methodologies, coupled with your influence, can help to position future Agile teams to avoid the most common traps that organizations encounter in their implementation of these methodologies.

As the adoption of Agile approaches grows and matures in your department, you can refine your use of Agile by enlisting qualified consultants, participating in online Agile forums, and reading Agile resources.

Over time, you may want to also consider providing staff with more formal guidance on adopting and applying Agile approaches. The IT industry has benefited greatly by having formal training and certification courses to teach people how to more effectively apply Agile methods (such as Scrum) in their software development projects.

Another key advantage is that, once Agile approaches are in place, the infrastructure needed to sustain these approaches is relatively small (mostly ongoing staff education and resource allocation to participate on Agile teams).

Added to these benefits is the fact that there is a groundswell of resources available for Agile teams to learn from the community of Agile practitioners who have been refining the approaches for the past 20 years (*see Chapter 21: More Information on Agile for a list of these resources*). So, even the costs of ongoing staff education can be reduced by leveraging the expertise (and generosity) of others in the Agile community who are working together to improve the processes for all organizations.

All of this means that introducing Agile approaches to other areas of your department – and your organization – can be a relatively low-cost activity with significant ongoing returns; and there is no one more qualified than you to make this happen.

Agile approaches have historically had a slow emergence in traditional organizations. Because they present a decidedly different way of working, much of the adoption of Agile approaches has been due to participants publicizing the exceptional results that they experienced – and then encouraging other areas of the organization to trial the approaches. In some cases, members of successful Agile teams have also strategically volunteered to work with other departments on their Agile projects, to enable them to directly benefit from their experience.

Adopting Agile approaches may seem like a radical shift for some organizations, but they have also been proven to produce radically improved outcomes for those who have. This is exactly why the effectiveness of Agile approaches needs to be promoted by the people who have benefited most from their success.

CHAPTER 21: MORE INFORMATION ON AGILE

The following are general, methodology-specific and practice-specific Agile sources that you can refer to for further information:

General information on Agile

Agile Alliance: *www.agilealliance.com*

Agile: An Executive Guide – Real results from IT budgets, Jamie Lynn Cooke, IT Governance Publishing (2011): *www.itgovernanceusa.com/product/2218.aspx*

AgileCanberra forum: *http://au.groups.yahoo.com/group/agilecanberra/*

Agile Journal: *www.agilejournal.com*

AgileKiwi – Practical Agile Software Development: *www.agilekiwi.com*

Agile Manifesto: *www.agilemanifesto.org*

AgileSoftwareDevelopment.com:
www.agilesoftwaredevelopment.com

Alistair Cockburn: *http://alistair.cockburn.us/*

*Fundamentals of Agile Project Management: An Overview
(Technical Manager's Survival Guides),* Gonçalves M,
Heda R, ASME Press (2010):
*www.amazon.com/Fundamentals-Agile-Project-
Management-
Technical/dp/0791802965/ref=sr_1_117?s=books&ie=UT
F8&qid=1297939406&sr=1-117*

The New Methodology
www.thoughtworks.com/articles/new-methodology

Specific Agile methodologies

Overview

A Practical Guide to Seven Agile Methodologies, Coffin R,
Lane D: Part one: *www.devx.com/architect/Article/32761*;
Part two: *www.devx.com/architect/Article/32836*

Scrum

Scrum Alliance: *www.scrumalliance.org*

Glossary of Scrum Terms, Szalvay V, Scrum Alliance, Inc. (2007):
www.scrumalliance.org/articles/39-glossary-of-scrum-terms

Scrum and Agile Presentations by Mike Cohn of Mountain Goat Software (various dates):
www.mountaingoatsoftware.com/presentations

DSDM

What is DSDM? Clifton M, Dunlap J (2003):
www.codeproject.com/KB/architecture/dsdm.aspx

DSDM Explained, Davies R, JAOO (2004):
www.agilexp.com/presentations/DSDMexplained.pdf

FDD™

An Overview of FDD™ – Web Development Methodology:
www.influxive.com/fdd-overview.html

Feature Driven Development™ (FDD™) and Agile Modeling, Ambler S W:
www.agilemodeling.com/essays/fdd.htm

21: More Information on Agile

Lean

Lean Primer, Larman C & Vodde B (2009): *www.leanprimer.com/downloads/lean_primer.pdf*

Leading Lean Software Development: Results Are Not the Point, Poppendieck.LLC (2009): *www.poppendieck.com/pdfs/LLSD_intro.pdf*

Running Agile: A Practitioner's View to Lean and Agile: http://runningagile.com/

XP

eXtreme Programming™*: a gentle introduction: www.extremeprogramming.org*

Kanban

Kanban (overview): *www.crisp.se/kanban*

Kanban and Scrum – making the most of both, Kniberg H and Skarin M (2010): *www.infoq.com/minibooks/kanban-scrum-minibook*

RUP®

IBM Rational Unified Process® (RUP®): *www-01.ibm.com/software/awdtools/rup*

21: More Information on Agile

Agile Modeling and the Rational Unified Process® (RUP®):

www.agilemodeling.com/essays/agileModelingRUP.htm

EssUP

Essential Practices:

www.ivarjacobson.com/uploadedFiles/Pages/Knowledge_C entre/Resources/Collateral/Resources/EssentialPractices2_ Brochure.pdf

AUP

The Agile Unified Process (AUP):

www.ambysoft.com/unifiedprocess/agileUP.html

Crystal

Crystal methodologies:

http://alistair.cockburn.us/Crystal+methodologies

Industry research on Agile

5th Annual State of Agile Development Survey 2010, VersionOne:

www.versionone.com/pdf/2010_State_of_Agile_Developme nt_Survey_Results.pdf

The state of application development in enterprises and SMBs: business data services North America and Europe, Stone J, Database and Network Journal (April 1st 2007):

www.thefreelibrary.com/The+state+of+application+develo pment+in+enterprises+and+SMBs:...-a0162832944

Selected Agile case studies

Agile Coaching in British Telecom, Meadows L and Hanly S (2006): *www.agilejournal.com/articles/columns/column-articles/144-agile-coaching-in-british-telecom*

Rolling out Agile in a Large Enterprise, Benefield G, Proceedings of the 41st Annual Hawaii International Conference on System Sciences (HICSS) (2008):

www.computer.org/portal/web/csdl/doi/10.1109/HICSS.200 8.382

Information on TQM and KAIZEN

Total Quality Management (TQM) – An Integrated Approach to Quality and Continuous Improvement, Kotelnikov V (last updated January 27th 2011)

www.1000ventures.com/business_guide/im_tqm_main.html

KAIZEN – The Japanese Strategy for Continuous Improvement, Kotelnikov V (last updated November 9th 2010):

www.1000ventures.com/business_guide/mgmt_kaizen_main .html

Information on Lean manufacturing

Common Questions Organizations Ask About Lean Manufacturing, Keberdle CF, Lean Solutions Group, LLC (2008):

www.leansolutionsgroup.com/images/Common_Questions_ About_Lean_Mfg.pdf

Lean Principles, Kilpatrick J, Utah Manufacturing Extension Partnership (2003): *http://mhc-net.com/whitepapers_presentations/LeanPrinciples.pdf*

ITG RESOURCES

IT Governance Ltd. sources, creates and delivers products and services to meet the real-world, evolving IT governance needs of today's organizations, directors, managers and practitioners. The ITG website (*www.itgovernance.co.uk*) is the international one-stop-shop for corporate and IT governance information, advice, guidance, books, tools, training and consultancy.

http://www.itgovernance.co.uk/project_governance.aspx is the page on our website for resources relevant to this book.

Other Websites

Books and tools published by IT Governance Publishing (ITGP) are available from all business booksellers and are also immediately available from the following websites:

www.itgovernance.co.uk/catalog/355 provides information and online purchasing facilities for every currently available book published by ITGP.

www.itgovernance.eu is our euro-denominated website which ships from Benelux and has a growing range of books in European languages other than English.

www.itgovernanceusa.com is a US$-based website that delivers the full range of IT Governance products to North America, and ships from within the continental US.

www.itgovernanceasia.com provides a selected range of ITGP products specifically for customers in South Asia.

www.27001.com is the IT Governance Ltd. website that deals specifically with information security management, and ships from within the continental US.

Pocket Guides

For full details of the entire range of pocket guides, simply follow the links at *www.itgovernance.co.uk/publishing.aspx*.

Toolkits

ITG's unique range of toolkits includes the IT Governance Framework Toolkit, which contains all the tools and guidance that you will need in order to develop and implement an appropriate IT governance framework for your organization. Full details can be found at *www.itgovernance.co.uk/ products/519*.

For a free paper on how to use the proprietary Calder-Moir IT Governance Framework, and for a free trial version of the toolkit, see *www.itgovernance.co.uk/calder_moir.aspx*.

There is also a wide range of toolkits to simplify implementation of management systems, such as an ISO/IEC 27001 ISMS or a BS25999 BCMS, and these can all be viewed and purchased online at: *www.itgovernance.co.uk/catalog/1*.

Best Practice Reports

ITG's range of Best Practice Reports is now at *www.itgovernance.co.uk/best-practice-reports.aspx*. These offer you essential, pertinent, expertly researched information on a number of key issues including Web 2.0 and Green IT.

ITG Resources

Training and Consultancy

IT Governance also offers training and consultancy services across the entire spectrum of disciplines in the information governance arena. Details of training courses can be accessed at *www.itgovernance.co.uk/training.aspx* and descriptions of our consultancy services can be found at *www.itgovernance.co.uk/consulting.aspx*. Why not contact us to see how we could help you and your organization?

Newsletter

IT governance is one of the hottest topics in business today, not least because it is also the fastest moving, so what better way to keep up than by subscribing to ITG's free monthly newsletter *Sentinel*? It provides monthly updates and resources across the whole spectrum of IT governance subject matter, including risk management, information security, ITIL® and IT service management, project governance, compliance and so much more. Subscribe for your free copy at: *www.itgovernance.co.uk/newsletter.aspx*.

EU for product safety is Stephen Evans, The Mill Enterprise Hub, Stagreenan, Drogheda, Co. Louth, A92 CD3D, Ireland. (servicecentre@itgovernance.eu)